MADAME HILLARY

MADAME HILLARY

THE DARK ROAD
TO THE WHITE HOUSE

R. EMMETT TYRRELL, JR.

WITH MARK W. DAVIS

Since 1947
REGNERY
PUBLISHING, INC.
An Eagle Publishing Company • Washington, DC

Library of Congress Cataloging-in-Publication Data

Tyrrell, R. Emmett.
  Madame Hillary : the dark road to the White House / R. Emmett Tyrrell and Mark W. Davis.
      p. cm.
Includes bibliographical references and index.
  ISBN 0-89526-067-0
  1. Clinton, Hillary Rodham. 2. Clinton, Hillary Rodham--Ethics. 3. Presidents' spouses—United States—Biography. 4. Women legislators—United States—Biography. 5. Legislators—United States—Biography. 6. United States. Congress. Senate—Biography. 7. United States—Politics and government—2001- 8. Presidents—United States—Election—2004. 9. United States—Politics and government—1993-2001. 10. Radicalism—United States. I. Davis, Mark W. (Mark William), 1955– II. Title.
  E887.C55T97 2004
  973.929'092—dc22

                          2003027009

Published in the United States by
Regnery Publishing, Inc.
An Eagle Publishing Company
One Massachusetts Avenue, NW
Washington, DC 20001

Visit us at www.regnery.com

Distributed to the trade by
National Book Network
4720-A Boston Way
Lanham, MD 20706

Printed on acid-free paper

Manufactured in the United States of America

10 9 8 7 6 5 4 3 2 1

Books are available in quantity for promotional or premium use. Write to Director of Special Sales, Regnery Publishing, Inc., One Massachusetts Avenue, NW, Washington, DC 20001, for information on discounts and terms, or call (202) 216-0600.

To the memory of Barbara Olson
and the presence of Ted Olson

CONTENTS

INTRODUCTION 1

CHAPTER ONE: Driving the Party....................................7

CHAPTER TWO: The Day Job 35

CHAPTER THREE: Livid History 67

CHAPTER FOUR: An Ideological Life 99

CHAPTER FIVE: The Coming Campaign 133

CHAPTER SIX: Fatal Attraction 161

CHAPTER SEVEN: The Presidency of Clinton 44 187

CHAPTER EIGHT: How to Defeat Hillary 201

ACKNOWLEDGMENTS 209

NOTES...213

INDEX 221

Introduction

This is a book about an ambitious, power-hungry woman—the wife of the forty-second president of the United States and a deep-dyed radical. She reminds me of the late Madame Mao, Jiang Qing. In China Madame Mao was called "the white-boned demon," after the legendary phantasm that could supposedly take on different shapes and was never more dangerous than when wearing a seductive guise. I see no diabolism in Madame Hillary, but I do see a Coat and Tie Radical—a phantasm who takes on the shape of respectability: wife, mother, first lady, senator from New York, all while harboring and insinuating the agenda of the radical left.

Many are fooled, but should not be. The dodge is a familiar one. It is how the left-wing radicals of the 1960s mastered their conquest of America's institutions—from academe to the Democratic Party. It is also Hillary Clinton's strategy as she plots her dark road to the White House.

In her book *Hell to Pay*, the late Barbara Olson described this radical milieu that gave rise to Hillary and her generational cohorts by quoting Danish philosopher Søren Kierkegaard: "A passionate, tumul-tuous age will overthrow everything, pull everything down; but a rev-olutionary age that is at the same time reflective and passionless leaves everything standing but cunningly empties it of significance."

Even in the passionate 1960s, Madame Hillary was first and fore-most concerned with maintaining her "political viability" (to use the now historic phrase the youthful Bill Clinton blurted out during his tireless struggle to evade the draft). She was not the kind of left-wing student who was going to blot her résumé by knocking off a bank, shooting a cop, or abandoning herself to sex, drugs, and rehab. She and her future husband were not bomb-throwing leftists but apple-polishing leftists. They were and remain creatures of ambition. Con-sequently, they would alternately fetch a left-wing professor's approbation with a radical feint, and then ingratiate themselves to corporate or grad-school interviewers by donning coat and tie (or the co-ed's equivalent).

Behind all the permutations of clothes and hair is Madame Hillary—a Hillary whose agenda comes from the fevered 1960s left: Peace! The environment! Equality! Minority rights! Sexual utopia! An end to the profit motive! Change, endless change! At one time or another, Hillary pursued all these enthusiasms and more, but always within safe confines, because she knew that it would not be easy in America to launch a new "Great Leap Forward."

She was certainly reminded of that truth when life with Bill took her to the Deep South. When she arrived in Arkansas wearing thick granny glasses, her hair greasy and swept back under a cheap head-band, her clothes sufficiently baggy to bring visions of left-wing pro-testers to the minds of patriotic Arkansans, it became apparent that her recent past could be problematic. She needed an antidote to rumors about her recent activism up in Yankeeland, which included her defense of the Black Panthers and her employment by a left-wing lawyer rumored to be a Stalinist. So what did Hillary do in her first year in Little Rock? She tried to enlist in the United States Marine Corps. That ought to establish her bona fides as a patriot! At the time, it was considered a preposterous thing for a young woman to do, but both Clintons have a penchant for grandstanding. Sometimes it works. Here is Hillary's story, in her own words.

So I walked into our local recruiting office, and I think it was just my bad luck that the person who happened to be there on duty could not have been older than twenty-one. He was in perfect physical shape. So I sat down and I said, you know, I wanted to explore—I didn't know whether I thought active duty would be a good idea, reserve, you know, maybe National Guard, something along those lines.

This young man looked at me and he said, "How old are you?"

I said, "Well, twenty-seven."...I had these really thick glasses on.

He said, "How bad's your eyesight?" I said, "It's pretty bad." And he said, "How bad?" So I told him. He said, "That's pretty bad."

And he finally said to me, he said, "You're too old. You can't see. And you're a woman." And then he went on...this man, young man, was a Marine. He said, "But maybe the dogs [the Army] would take you."[1]

Distracting Arkansans from the radicalism of her youth was only one reason for Hillary's visit with the Marine recruiter. A former radical, a woman who cut her teeth in many of the same movements as Hillary Clinton, offers a second reason. "It's called 'walking through,'" this ex-radical says. The term is lifted from Mao Zedong, who spoke of his "long march" through existing institutions. "There are those who fight to overthrow the system," the former radical says. "Then there are those who walk through the system, undermining it, subverting it from within. Hillary's always been one to walk through. She walked through as a governor's wife, as first lady, now the Senate."

The question to be answered is: Where is Senator Hillary Clinton walking to? The answer might frighten you. Madame Hillary, the ultimate Coat and Tie Radical, remains a revolutionary. Her goal is to "leave everything standing but cunningly empty it of significance"—or at least significance as most Americans understand it. A Marine Corps uniform with Hillary inside it would have been a Marine Corps uniform emptied of significance. Also emptied of significance by Madame Hillary and her husband, Boy Clinton, are the original intent of the Constitution, the meaning of perjury, the meaning of adultery, even the meaning of the word "is."

Of course, Madame Hillary does not empty our existing institutions merely to create a vacuum. She has an agenda with which to fill them.

Like Madame Mao, the white-boned demon, Madame Hillary, the country's stern and well-coiffed self-appointed nanny, controls an enormous personal and political machine. Working together, the Clintons now manage the Democratic Party as their personal prefecture, weeding out weak candidates where they need the party to be strong and puffing up Manchurian candidates when they need someone to clear a path.

When Andrew Cuomo's mounting failures became an embarrassment to New York Democrats, Bill Clinton smoothed the way for his dignified departure. When Louisiana senator Mary Landrieu faced imminent defeat after alienating African-Americans, Bill Clinton called black ministers and shored her up. When the roguish Al Sharpton jumped into the Democratic presidential primary, threatening to congeal the African-American vote into an alienated bloc, the Clintonistas persuaded disgraced former senator Carol Moseley Braun to mount a bid that was equally preposterous, and equally useful in keeping the black vote fluid. When Dr. Howard Dean, a Democrat unbeholden to the Clintons, threatened to run away with the nomination and undo the Clintons' political kingdom, the Clintonistas dispatched General Wesley Clark, the ideal Manchurian candidate. His gaffes and idiocies ensure the planned obsolescence of his campaign, but not before he undertakes his search-and-destroy mission to blow the tires out of the Dean machine.

But this is not all. Senator Clinton chairs the Democratic Steering and Coordination Committee, where she can wield intimidating power over her colleagues, blocking or advancing their committee assignments. Clinton servitors are all over the Democratic Party, including Hillary's handpicked moneyman, Terry McAuliffe, the chairman of the Democratic National Committee. Clinton lackeys fill the hierarchies of the labor unions, the Democratic Party's most reliable source of votes, organizational muscle, and money. They are setting up think tanks and political action committees, and working to fund an explicitly liberal radio and television network. They also include a shadowy little army of private investigators and other cretinous, thuggish, "opposition research" figures, people the Clintons have used in the past to perfect the politics of personal destruction and to kill off the candidacies of opponents—a group the press has been slow to investigate.[2] And, of course, Madame Hillary and her celebrity husband have become one of the largest sources of money for a party that now, thanks to its own campaign finance reform, is starving for cash.

In short, Madame Hillary has indirect control or deep and unparalleled influence over *all* the major elements of the Democratic Party's infrastructure:

- Its campaign cash
- Its labor battalions
- Its ideas
- Its media
- And, to an astonishing extent, its very candidates for the presidency.

Hillary is now on the brink of perhaps the most astonishing takeover in American history. To achieve it, she will pursue a generational battle pitting the Coat and Tie Radicals of the 1960s against her generational *bête noir*, that is to say, the penny-loafer conservatives, exemplified by George W. Bush, who in his collegiate days preferred beer-bashing to raids on the dean's office, intramural sports to protests at Wellesley, and the practicality of Harvard Business School to remaking the world through lessons learned at Yale Law School. That battle now continues, its opposing sides more mature and seasoned, and its outcome will determine America's future.

Longtime Hillary watcher Mark W. Davis and I have investigated Madame Hillary and her designs on the country and plans for the presidency. What follows is our report. Read it and be warned.

CHAPTER ONE

Driving the Party

Power is not static; it cannot be frozen
and preserved like food; it must grow or die.[1]

—Saul Alinsky

"THIS IS A WOMAN WHO'S BEEN FIRST LADY, who's lived in the White House and shared power with a president," says one of Hillary's Senate colleagues. "The Senate itself is too casual, the power is too diffuse, for her to be happy. Her ambition is not the Senate leadership."

He thinks a moment, and adds, "Senators are posturing all the time. It's different with Hillary. Her ambitions are different than getting reelected. It's obvious she has a much greater goal in mind. Her ambition is the White House, with all the moves to prepare the way."

Throughout 2003, Hillary weighed her options. The coming presidential election presented her with agonizingly difficult political choices. But she has faced such choices before.

"The most brilliant decision the Clintons ever made was to get into the 1992 race when they did," says a major national political correspondent who has covered both Clintons. "In 1991, all the quality candidates stayed out of it, thinking that [the first] President Bush was unbeatable. The Clintons shrewdly picked a time to run when the [Democratic] field was open. All the reporting has it that she was the one who told Bill, 'You can take this guy. You've got to go now.'"

After deciding to launch Bill toward the presidency in 1991, Hillary made another shrewd decision in 1999. Listening to Susan Thomases, a longtime adviser, Hillary decided to run for the Senate, and not from Arkansas, but from New York, where big media and big money come together. Four years later, Senator Hillary was surrounded by people telling her the same things she had once told Bill, things like, "the second President Bush is another paper tiger." They reminded her that Gore beat Bush by 539,947 votes in the popular tally. Bush, they said, is suffering from jobless recovery syndrome and Iraqi fever. In short, "Hillary, go for it!"

You can take this guy. You've got to go now.

The election of 2004 presented Hillary with a painful dilemma. She knew that she has two shots at national office, in 2004, when she will be fifty-seven years old, and in 2008, when she will be sixty-one (her birthday is October 26, 1947). By 2012, Hillary will be sixty-five. She has to expect that by that time there will be some rust on the wings of her celebrity. Younger, newer stars will be rising in the Democratic Party. Throughout 2003, she waffled: Which year to run, 2004 or 2008? It had to be one or the other. The days of William Jennings Bryan's and Adlai Stevenson's repeated campaigns for the nomination are gone. Candidates these days are allowed only one shot at the top of the ticket.

Even during the first Democratic primaries, donors and political heavy hitters around the country were importuning Hillary to jump

into the race. On the East Coast, Clinton henchman Harold Ickes—
the former White House deputy chief of staff and Democratic Party
bagman, the organizer of the Clintons' reckless fund-raising efforts of
1996, and the architect of Hillary's Senate victory—was once again at
work clearing the way. He organized what *BusinessWeek* called a
"shadow party," a planned $250 million machine operating outside of
the McCain-Feingold restrictions on campaign spending, directing
millions of soft dollars from unions and trial lawyers to "issue ads."[2]

In California, the signals were more ambiguous. The powerful Hollywood donor base split into two factions. One camp, represented by
director Rob Reiner, originally gravitated to Vermont governor
Howard Dean, but soon came to fear that the Green Mountain governor—and greenhorn candidate—could not go all the way. This group
of liberal purists, personified by Barbra Streisand and actors Ed Begley, Jr. and Martin Sheen, implored Hillary to be prepared to jump into
the race. They pointed to a 2003 Quinnipiac University survey showing Hillary with 42 percent of the Democratic vote, giving her a mas-
sive base against the rest of the Democratic presidential pack, all of
whom could command only single-digit or low double-digit support.

Another camp was led by mega-producer David Geffen, who along
with partners Steven Spielberg and Jeffrey Katzenberg is particularly
close to Bill Clinton. The three once discussed with the former president the possibility of hiring him for the board of their studio,
DreamWorks SKG. The Geffen camp held that Hillary should cool her
heels, as the party is destined to lose this time around. "The Geffen
faction is telling Hillary that to run this time and lose makes her seriously tarnished goods," said one prominent Hollywood producer in
the summer of 2003. "And these people don't do anything without
talking to Bill Clinton and Terry McAuliffe. At the same time, they

worried that no one was catching fire. So there is mass confusion on the presidential level," the producer reported. "Everyone is searching for a winner. Even big producers wet their pants to be able to pick up the phone and say, 'Hello, Mr. President.' It really jazzes them. But who's it going to be? The true believers will continue to hold out hope someone will break out, but they won't spend their PR capital. In this town, driven by image, everyone wants to be on the winning ticket. So Hollywood is in a quandary. Major performance artists are not doing big concerts, major stars are not opening their Malibu homes to fundraisers."

Then California had an earthquake—the "Arnold" earthquake, a 7.1 on the political Richter scale. Democrats speak bravely of Arnold Schwarzenegger's raid on California governor Gray Davis's job as a sign that the public is in a mood to recall incumbents. They gamely predict Bush will be next. Seasoned politicos in both parties privately say that this is so much whistling past the graveyard. The election of Governor Schwarzenegger will force Democrats to divert millions of dollars from swing states won by Gore with razor-thin margins merely to secure California, a state Democrats previously considered a "lock."

To make the decision even clearer for Hillary, the economy began to pick up steam in 2004, the job market improved, Dean started breaking out of the pack, and President Bush's poll numbers firmed up after fading—showing that the trust forged in the fires of September 11, 2001, is surprisingly durable. 2008 is, at this writing, still her likeliest option. But until late 2003, Hillary herself did not know which path she would choose. She maintained a cool poker face, for all the cards she held were very good.

Behind her adamant public stand against running for president, Hillary asked her supporters to keep their wallets closed to the other candidates. She went further, actively diverting money from them. In August 2003, while Senator John Kerry was raising money in Southampton, Hillary was almost literally alongside him on Long Island, in nearby East Hampton, raising money hand over fist.[3] On September 7, 2003, Hillary, Bill, and Harold Ickes met with 150 of the crème de la crème of Democratic strategists and donors at the Clinton homestead in Chappaqua, New York, to stoke the fires of speculation. Bill spoke pointedly of there being "two stars" in the Democratic Party, Hillary and Wesley Clark (by implication relegating Howard Dean, Kerry, and Richard Gephardt to the role of "chopped liver"). "We might have another candidate or two jumping into the race," the former president said, in another hint as broad as a carnie's wink.[4]

The Clintons, of course, later demurred when questions came in from the press. They had been misinterpreted, they said. Bill, one of his loyal mouthpieces told the *New York Times*, had temporarily forgotten about the Twenty-second Amendment, which forbids him from running again—as if it were possible for a former president to forget such a thing. Still, guests were adamant about what they had heard. One said that the people present "were not hallucinating. In the climate of heightened interest in a candidacy, they know they need to be extra, extremely careful with their language."[5] While Hillary denied any interest in running—and dramatized her quasi-Sherman stance by taking adulatory appeals from supportive groups off her website— Bill kept dropping unsubtle hints. He told a California audience, "I was impressed at the state fair in New York, which is in Republican country in upstate New York, at how many New Yorkers came up and said they would release her from her commitment if she wanted to do it."[6] Of course, eliciting and staging appeals to run is exactly how

Governor Bill Clinton, fresh from a reelection campaign, wiggled out of a pledge not to run for the White House. He was setting up the means for Hillary to also renege and run in 2004, as he had reneged and run in 1992.

"All this attention, if she didn't want it, she could stop it," says one reporter who covers her. "These things keep popping up, like the *New York Times* article on their Chappaqua meeting. They knew that would get out."

Such machinations (and these are just the visible ones) show that Hillary surveyed the field like a general wondering when to go to battle, checking the weather updates and watching the changing position of the opposing army. When the "facts on the ground" are so alarmingly ambiguous, most politicians err on the side of caution. It is a testament to the near-total control the Clintons have over the Democratic Party that Hillary—an undeclared candidate—could keep every conceivable option open for as long as she needed.

But what were her best options? Hillary and her people identified three.

The first option could be called Bide and Build, or Wait for 2008—the favorite of most Democrats and the "smart money" on Washington's K Street, lobbyists' row. After all, Bush's approval ratings through the second half of 2003 held in the mid-fifties. Though these levels fell from their stratospheric wartime highs, the fall itself reveals a natural base for Bush. In fact, President Bush's ratings in the polls track those of President Clinton at the end of his first term, before he went on to best Bob Dole.

So Hillary could bide her time and build her chances—not of winning the nomination, because that is likely hers for the taking—but of winning the presidency when she does run. If she racks up a convincing victory in her 2006 reelection to the Senate, that will go a long way toward establishing her in the public mind as an authentic political leader, not just a celebrity who got elected in a fluke election. Hillary can build on her critique of Republicans on health care and homeland security. She can realistically hope that four more years of Republican dominance will begin to wear. And she can profit from a total collapse of the Democratic Party in 2004, after which she might emerge as leader of the opposition.

But there are dangers with this first option. What if Rudy Giuliani knocks her out of the Senate in 2006? A Marist College Institute poll in fall 2003 found that Giuliani would crush her, 57 percent to 40 percent. That same poll found that 69 percent of New Yorkers do not want her to run for president in 2004, up 15 percent from April 2003. As a senatorial loser, she might still be able to win the presidency; after all, Lincoln did it. But that would be unlikely. Sorry, Hillary, but you are no Abe Lincoln. Just as bad for her, what if the 2004 Democratic nominee actually *wins*? Then President Hillary remains a feminist fantasy. She cannot run against a Democratic incumbent seeking reelection in 2008. If 2012 were still a viable year for her, she would be a senior citizen facing an incumbent vice president for the nomination.

The second option could be called Settling for Second Best. As we shall see, Hillary championed the entry of certain candidates in the race for the 2004 nomination. It might not be difficult for the Clintons to persuade a John Edwards or a Wesley Clark to choose the woman who launched their political careers as a running mate. "There's this legend about Edwards being a successful lawyer who, on his own accord, decided to run for the Senate," says a longtime observer of North Carolina politics. "In fact, Edwards was Hillary's protégé. She recruited him from the beginning. She hated Lauch

Faircloth, and she knew Edwards through the trial lawyers' association." Faircloth had been an ally of the duke of Southern conservatism, Jesse Helms. How had he earned a place in Hillary's crosshairs? In her memoir, she blames Faircloth for having joined forces with Jesse Helms in a now-famous lunch to persuade another North Carolinian, Judge David Sentelle, to replace independent counsel Robert Fiske with Kenneth Starr.

General Wesley Clark, political naïf that he showed himself to be early in the campaign, was unguardedly candid with the press when he admitted Hillary had encouraged him to run. It was not long before Clark's campaign was abounding with Clintonistas: Clinton spokesman Mark Fabiani, Clinton presidential library president Skip Rutherford, Clinton UN ambassador Richard Sklar, Clinton White House aide Matt Bennett, and some genuine heavy hitters, like former secretary of commerce Mickey Kantor, top campaign aide Eli Segal, and Bruce Lindsey, the quiet, loyal cleanup man who dutifully tidied one mess after another in the wake of the Boy President.

The Clintons' fingerprints are so apparent on the Clark campaign that Hillary's mortal enemy, Rudy Giuliani, early on speculated in public that Clark was nothing but a stalking horse for Hillary. On a radio interview, he said that if one of the Democratic candidates "starts to emerge with the ability of being able to defeat President Bush, then I think she may just jump in."[7]

Both Edwards and Clark make good political matches for Hillary. In an Edwards/Clinton ticket, or a Clinton/Edwards ticket, one would have the match of two telegenic lawyers, one from New York, the other from North Carolina, both close to their African-American constituents and sharing the same liberal judicial views. In Wesley Clark, you would have the national security ticket combined with Hillary fresh from her work on the Armed Services Committee and homeland security.

Of all the candidates, Clark is the most pliable. Though President Bill Clinton had approved the general's removal from the top NATO post, the Clinton camp put out the face-saving story that the president had been misled by the Pentagon, and had acquiesced in the move without fully understanding what was up. Bill has praised Clark for having "a sackful of guts." Clintons' people fanned rumors in September that the only person Clark would consider for the second spot would be Hillary. The rumors became so heated that Bill and Hillary had to cool things down by publicly and privately mollifying the other candidates with expressions of neutrality.

In both the Edwards and Clark candidacies, Hillary is not only keeping her second option open. She is also keeping the other candidates humble—and in a state of confusion. With the arrival of candidate Clark, Kerry lost the ability to brag that he was the only candidate who had actually seen combat. Lieberman lost much of his centrist appeal. Edwards and the soon-to-retire Bob Graham saw their claim on the South diminished. Hillary sent Clark into the race in the same spirit as a computer hacker sending out viruses, with the intention to disrupt, to discombobulate, and to keep others from rising to the top. This is why, when Clark catapulted ahead of the other candidates in the polls, Hillary called David Geffen in October 2003 and told him, according to our well-placed Hollywood source, to give his money to Clark. She added, "But if Clark doesn't catch on, we may have to reconsider our strategy."

Still, Howard Dean remained problematic for Hillary through 2003. Dean is a serious threat to the Clintons because he adumbrates a new power base in the Democratic Party. He is independent of the Clintons'

base, that golden triangle of special interests; ambitious, amoral candidates; and prosperous power brokers like Democratic National
Committee chairman Terry McAuliffe and the Clintons themselves. In
stark contrast, Dean sparked his campaign with the excitement of
young (often first-time) voters and multitudes of small donors on the
Internet. Dean is the first candidate of the post-television campaign
era; his is the first national campaign in cyberspace.

Dean himself is a flinty, antagonistic man, with whom I debated
for several years on a television show called *The Editors*, taped in Mon-
treal. We spent hours together and went head to head on the show. In
those days, the mid- and late 1990s, Dean was a well-programmed
Clinton defender. It was ironic to see him becoming a threat to the
Clintons' control of the Democratic Party in 2003. Still, based on my
experiences with Dean, the hostility is understandable. Dr. Howard
Dean is easily riled. He is very competitive, and once his prickly ego is
agitated by almost any kind of opposition it is unlikely he will back
off. Rather, he will barge ahead, as he did in debate with me, shooting
his mouth off in facile, barbed, but ultimately ill-conceived pronun-
ciamentos; giving no ground; creating a donnybrook where reasoned
discourse plays better. I have no doubt that the hostility between him
and the Clintons is real and that it is a threat to Hillary. His campaign
might even tap into principled Democrats' desire to rid the party of
the Clintons' sleaziness. Once nominated, however, Dean will need the
wealth and apparatus of the current Democratic Party behind him,
and it is conceivable that he might cut a deal with the power brokers
and choose the most famous woman in the world as his running
mate. When I faced him on *The Editors* I recognized that, beneath all
the "good doctor" attitudinizing, he was a conventional political oper-
ator, which explained his instinctive defense of his fellow Democrat

in the White House. He is also a little rash; he wanted to challenge Vice President Al Gore for the nomination in 2000.

Most Democratic operatives dismiss the idea of Hillary serving as vice president for any Democratic candidate, but at least one prominent Democrat running for president has been worried about it. A high-level campaign aide privately fretted that his boss (then considering the second-tier spot himself) would be knocked out of consideration for veep if Hillary decides to settle for second best.

"She can't take the risk that a Democrat can win in '04 without her," this campaign operative said. "She's definitely going to be on the ticket, there's a lot of talk about her as vice president."

Being a political chess player, however, Hillary has to think many moves ahead. What if she runs as vice president and loses? The nomination for the second spot could enhance her standing as it once did Joseph Lieberman's. It could also destroy her future in politics, as it did Geraldine Ferraro's. All would be dependent on whether Hillary was judged the bright spot on a losing ticket or the cause of its demise. Running and losing also runs the risk of alienating New York voters two years before Hillary has to run for reelection to the Senate.

What if a Democratic ticket featuring Hillary as the vice presidential candidate wins? It is this possibility that causes Washington's insiders to discount the possibility that she would accept second place. No one doubts Hillary's desire to sit in the Oval Office; would she, however, accept playing second fiddle for up to eight years?

Hillary has a history of accepting subordinate positions and using them to undermine institutions from the inside or from below. She did this as first lady of Arkansas, as we will see, as an appointee to the board of the Legal Services Corporation, and—most famously—as first lady of the United States. Moreover, as veep on a winning

Democratic ticket, she would be next in line, only a heartbeat away from the big job.

The third option Hillary weighed in 2003 could be called Divide and Conquer. The Clintons recruited several of the current Democratic candidates in order to keep the field even and open. "There's the potential for her to take it," said a Republican senator. "If Wesley Clark gets in, and you have nine or ten Democrats, with three of them running strong and even to the end, it's not inconceivable you could have a deadlocked convention."

Bill and Hillary added to the weakness of the field by taking every opportunity to generate news, to leach publicity and excitement from anything the declared presidential candidates did. Hillary did this with her tireless summer book tour, gaining more attention than all the other Democrats combined. Bill diverted attention from the Democratic presidential aspirants when he was not with them, creating news that distracted rank-and-file Democrats from the campaigning candidates. When he was with them, he was even more of a distraction.

"Bill Clinton definitely hurts the Democratic presidential candidates, keeping them in the wings," said a national political correspondent. "When he goes to the Iowa steak fry, he's the rock star making the rounds." The other candidates, by implication, are forced to stand in quiet admiration, looking like Clinton groupies. If the Clintons continue to weaken the field, at the right moment, Hillary might succumb to a "draft" and take over the nomination.

Most Democratic operatives and political observers say that such a thing is flatly impossible. They point to the filing deadlines Hillary has missed for one important primary after another. "After what happened in Florida, you can't rule anything out," said Ed Kilgore, a Democratic operative and expert in Southern politics. But he called the idea that Hillary could take the nomination "a conservative fantasy." "Over half the delegates could be pledged by March, all by the nomination," he said.

Throughout the primary season, another line of thinking held that anything is possible in the Democratic Party in the Age of Clinton.

One top former Reagan strategist says, "We'll know by March 2 who the nominee is," agreeing with Kilgore that the Super Tuesday mega-primary would settle the nomination. Perhaps the matter will be firmly settled by the time you read this. What remains of enduring significance is that, regardless of which path Hillary ultimately chooses, she had the drive and the power to make certain it was still possible for her to get into the race. She has kept open the maximum number of options. She was still actively considering a presidential campaign well past the point when it would have seemed impossible.

How might a convention takeover be engineered? Contested conventions rely on fragmented loyalties among delegates. Fragmentation is possible because of the number of candidates with relatively equal representation, and the fact that the Democrats—unlike the Republicans—do not run winner-take-all primaries. It is possible that two or three Democrats will go to Boston with relatively equal shares of delegates. Out of such chaos, a surprised and demure Hillary could accept the nomination in the face of deafening demand for her from the convention floor, where delegates may be committed to Dean or Kerry first time around, but would bolt for Hillary after that.

America has not enjoyed a truly contested convention since 1952, when Adlai Stevenson won the nomination on the third ballot. The last time a nomination was really at stake on the convention floor was 1960, when the primary process of that time allowed John F. Kennedy too few delegates to dismiss the opposition of Lyndon Johnson,

Stuart Symington, and Adlai Stevenson. The Democratic convention of 1968 was "contested" outside in the streets of Chicago. The Republican convention of 1976 and the Democratic convention of 1980 were at least dramatic, thanks to the tensions between the camps of Gerald Ford and Ronald Reagan, and of Jimmy Carter and Edward Kennedy.

Since then, conventions have tended to be national showcases for bad music, cliché-ridden rhetoric, and anchors competing to be the most portentous. But astute observers wondered if things would change in Boston at the 2004 Democratic convention. A former Reagan strategist, after confidently predicting a Democratic nominee in March, stops in mid-sentence to add, "unless it fragments all over the place. This thing is so front-loaded. But fragmentation is possible."

There are two relevant trends in modern Democratic nomination politics that most observers have overlooked. One is the recent willingness of the Democrats to discard the rules and manipulate candidacies. By the old rules, Hillary Clinton should never have been able to run for a Senate seat from New York. Representative Nita Lowey had already laid claim to the seat of the retiring Daniel Patrick Moynihan. That did not keep Hillary from seizing her main chance (as another celebrity carpetbagger, Bobby Kennedy, had done three decades earlier). Lowey protested meekly, but found that her grip on the party establishment and donor base was too weak to withstand Hillary's queenly power of eminent domain.

In the New Jersey senate race in 2002, when it became apparent at the eleventh hour that the corrupt Robert Torricelli could not be reelected, the Democrats simply sent him to the showers while pulling retired senator Frank Lautenberg from the benches (a brazenly illegal action despite an acquiescent ruling from the state's liberal supreme court). In 2000, when Missouri governor Mel Carnahan was killed in a plane crash shortly before the election, it was deemed politically smart to keep the dead man on the ballot, and the Democrats did precisely that. When Senator Paul Wellstone was killed in a plane crash shortly before the 2002 election, again Democrats rewrote the rules and replaced him with former vice president Walter Mondale. There is no reason to doubt that Democrats will manipulate the rules once again, if it suits those in power.

So who are those in power in the Democratic Party? This question leads us to the other trend in modern Democratic politics, the Clintons' near total control over every aspect of the Democratic Party.

By the time you read this, Hillary's three options will likely be a moot issue. The point is that in late 2003, Hillary was still holding out, still contemplating taking the nomination in one form or another in case Bush slipped on a banana peel. This alone is proof of her startling ability to manipulate the party. What was once the party of Roosevelt and Truman is now very much the party of Clinton and Clinton.

The Clinton Mystique

How do two people control the oldest and largest democratic party in the country? What are their levers of control? On the surface, of course, it is their extraordinary appeal. Bill Clinton remains a mesmerizing figure to those he does not thoroughly repel. He still brings out the crowds, generating excitement like no former president since Teddy Roosevelt. No other ex-president has ever been such an inexhaustible ham. What is more, no white politician has ever developed a stronger hold on the loyalties of African-American voters than Bill Clinton.

Hillary's appeal, by contrast, is almost metaphysical. She represents the transcendent dreams of the feminist, the gay rights advocate, the eco-activist. But she also connects with the murky dreams of millions of suburban women who quietly enter the ballot booth and assert their independence from their family's party affiliation—just as Hillary's mother, along with innumerable other women, probably voted for John F. Kennedy in secret while her husband voted for Richard M. Nixon. Hillary's coalition is unprecedented, a linkage of moderate, suburban women and left-wing advocates.

The fascination that the Clintons exert over multitudes of Democrats and independents (and even some Republican women) represents their greatest visible lever of control over their party. But there are other levers, the most important of which is the lever releasing vast quantities of money.

The Clintons are a money machine, as is President Bush. In the third quarter of 2003, the president raised almost $50 million, more than triple the money raised by top Democrats. The Democratic Senate and House campaign committees are another story. Throughout 2003, they were running on fumes. The Democratic state parties, accustomed to large grants from the national Democratic Party, found themselves begging for money.

The reason for their sudden penury is the McCain-Feingold law, the so-called campaign finance reform, a useful rhetorical cudgel against the Republicans until President Bush called the Democrats' bluff and signed it into law. Now the cudgel is turned on them. Throughout the Clinton years, Democrats could rely on unlimited, "soft-dollar" donations that came in regular intervals and gigantic sums from individual trial lawyers, labor unions, liberal trust-fund babies, and Hollywood moguls. Thanks to McCain-Feingold, most of this soft-dollar largesse is off-limits to the official organs of the Democratic Party. Individuals may donate no more than $2,000 apiece. In this environment of limited, "hard-dollar" fund-raising, Republicans thrive. Often seen as the party of fat cats, Republicans do a far better job of eliciting a stream of $40 donations from the middle class and persuading wealthier Republicans to "max out."

While the Democratic campaign committees wander a barren landscape, looking for clumps of grass to eat, the Clintons preside over a lush oasis. They no longer have the Lincoln Bedroom to sell, but they do have the glamour of a $2.8 million neo-Georgian mansionette on Whitehaven, a short, elegant street just off Embassy Row in Washington, D.C. There, fund-raising events are executed with precision and professionalism, and the street is regularly clogged with jet black Lincoln Town Cars and the war wagons of the Secret Service. The Clintons also have their $1.7 million three-story Dutch colonial in suburban Chappaqua, New York, that potential donors will pay to see. These "home-raisers" occur, on average, about once a week. And, of course, for a few thousand dollars the Clintons will also offer the splendor of their presence. Many people, not otherwise political, will pay to meet Bill and Hill, much as fans line up for hours to catch a glimpse of Ben and J. Lo.

Making it all the sweeter is control of her namesake HILLPAC, a phenomenally successful "leadership" political action committee engorged with her Whitehaven funds—a type of PAC usually associated with senior leadership figures like Tom Daschle and Tom DeLay. During the 2002 election cycle, Hillary was among the Senate's top donors, disbursing more than $1 million to candidates (including more than one hundred members of Congress) and to party committees. In the 2002 cycle, she actively helped raise funds for more than thirty House and Senate candidates. With each donation she invests, Hillary strengthens her hold over Democratic officeholders.

"Who's going to raise that kind of money for the Democratic Party?" asks a senatorial colleague of Hillary's. "Not a Nancy Pelosi or a Dianne Feinstein. She's doling it out and she's getting the chits."

Her New York Senate colleague, Chuck Schumer, makes an interesting comparison. Schumer, no slouch, raises more than two-thirds of his money from within New York, with Wall Street and real estate interests leading the way. Hillary raises almost half of her funds from outside the state, with trial lawyers and law firms as her top categories. (She endearingly bestows the title "Hill Raisers" on those who collect large sums for her. Lesser mortals can log on to the Friends of Hillary website and become "Hill's Angels" for as little as $25.) Hillary has raised more than $31 million from the formal beginning of her independent political career through 2002.

Hillary raises so much money, in fact, that she can be the patroness of the Democratic Party while still spending the lion's share of her money on the care and feeding of her own staff, office, travel, direct mail, and political consultants. In 2002, 31 percent of the money her committee raised was spent to help Democratic candidates. In the first half of 2003, that percentage dropped to 21 percent.[8] Deborah Orin of the *New York Post* was the first to note that Hillary's political action committee, HILLPAC, and her personal campaign committee, Friends of Hillary, could make her a fund-raising double-dipper. Her two committees have the same address, the same sixteen staffers, and pay the same communications consultant. A donor could give money to both committees, and thereby double his legal contribution to Hillary.[9] Hillary also kept a soft-dollar committee, HILLPAC-N.Y., on idle, before the U.S. Supreme Court upheld the campaign finance law.

The size of HILLPAC's budget has allowed Hillary to capture and keep the best operators in the Democratic Party. "Certain offices have strong reputations for quality staff," says one high-ranking Senate Democratic aide of Hillary's Capitol Hill staff. "She has one of the best on the Hill, right up there with Kennedy and Moynihan." The same could be said for the people who run HILLPAC. A Republican insider continues this thought. "You can pick a good press secretary any time—all you need is the right chemistry. But at HILLPAC you see the hard-to-find staff—for instance, people who can manage travel at a presidential level. She's soaked up all this high-level talent, keeping this army fed and under her banner. It will make a strong skeletal organization for 2008."

Hillary knows how to match the inside game of legislative manipulation with the outside game of matching needy donors with vulnerable senators. She can do this because HILLPAC neatly dovetails with Hillary's official responsibilities as the chair of the Senate Democrats' Steering and Coordination Committee, the place where internal policy development comes together with the special interests that make up the Democratic Party.

The public face of the Clinton money machine is Terry McAuliffe, the upstate New Yorker who after becoming Bill Clinton's jovial golf buddy was elevated by the Clintons to lead the Democratic National Committee (DNC). McAuliffe is a Clinton loyalist of heroic proportions, having offered at the end of the Clinton presidency (when the Boy President was in hock owing to his Whitewater and impeachment legal bills) to pledge more than one million dollars to help the Clintons secure a mortgage for Hillary's Chappaqua homestead. Once ensconced in the DNC, McAuliffe fell under the same kind of scrutiny that has dogged the Clintons going back to the discovery of Hillary's cattle futures bonanza. In McAuliffe's case, the press discovered that in the 1990s he transformed an investment of $100,000 in Global Crossing into an $18 million profit. The fact that Global Crossing went belly up, putting thousands out of work, after making the DNC chairman a multimillionaire was problematic for McAuliffe, though it did not stifle him from linking the Bush administration to Enron and other 1990s business busts.

What has, however, really damaged McAuliffe is his failure at the ultimate Clintonian test of success. He performed abysmally in 2002, managing to lose seats to Republicans in an off-year election that should traditionally bring more seats to the party out of power. Then he transformed himself into a figure of fun by declaring this rout to be a "victory." Still worse, McAuliffe's legendary fund-raising ability is now constrained by the limits of McCain-Feingold. Nonetheless, McAuliffe is the Clintons' public right-hand man. Until he is replaced, he will dutifully keep a watchful eye over the party for the Clintons.

Meanwhile, the real money is being quietly raised by the Clintons' left-hand man, Harold Ickes. Unlimited money can, of course, be raised for non-official institutions, provided they engage in the selling of an issue and not a candidate, and refrain from directly coordinating with a campaign. Consequently, clever fellows like Ickes set up committees outside the Democratic Party, where they raise unlimited money to promote Democratic issues—universal health care, more teachers in the classroom, expansion of Medicare to people at age fifty-five—all funded, say, by a repeal of the Bush tax cuts. "Welcome to campaign finance reform," is how Ickes characterized his efforts to a reporter—efforts that can only advance Hillary.

Welcome to campaign finance reform, indeed. Such will be the tactics of what is expected to become a $250 million behemoth political organization called America Votes. It will be a federation of liberal interest groups that will target voters in such swing states as New Mexico, Florida, and Iowa. America Votes will rely on shared polling data, research, and mailing lists, including "Demzilla"—the data bank on voters maintained by the Democratic National Committee. Ickes—the same man Justice Department prosecutor Charles LaBella wanted to indict as the "Svengali" of the Clinton fund-raising scandals—will personally oversee a $50 million media campaign. How will he coordinate with the Democratic nominee? Ickes, with typical candor, told *BusinessWeek*, "It doesn't take much to figure out what the issues are and the messages you need to be helpful."[10] Another part of the effort will be Americans Coming Together, a $75 million "get-out-the-vote" effort started with a $10 million grant from billionaire George Soros, the émigré champion of legalized marijuana and a man with a peculiar mania against President George W. Bush.

With Ickes working behind the scenes, the left hand coordinates the money of the rising stealth Democratic Party, while the right hand, McAuliffe, manages the diminished role of the official party. Playing a key role at America Votes is AFL-CIO president John Sweeney, a certified Friend of Hillary who husbands the powers of America's declining labor movement. Certain also to play a role is another FOH, Gerald McEntee, the head of the American Federation of State, County, and Municipal Employees. This union is one of the few sectors of the labor movement that is actually growing: government workers. "Working with the unions," says one high-ranking Bush administration official, "I've lost all respect for them. The more

I work with them, the more they look like organized crime." When one union lost a regulatory appeal, a top union official told the Bush administration, "Well, we'll just have to go back to the baseball bat." They may be goons, but they are Hillary's goons.

If labor represents the crowbar and cleaver at the low end of Democratic politics, a newly founded think tank, the Center for American Progress, represents the high end, where ideas and policies come together. Headed by John Podesta, Bill Clinton's former chief of staff, the Center is strategically placed adjacent to the K Street power corridor, with the help of a reported $20 million donation from Soros the Munificent. (Dare we call him Richard Mellon Soros?) It is designed to match the intellectual firepower of the libertarian Cato Institute and the deep policy impact of the conservative Heritage Foundation.

The Center is divided between a 501(c)3—the tax status of a non-partisan think tank—and a 501(c)4, a designation that allows the propaganda section to be more aggressively partisan.

Sarah Wartell, a veteran of the Clinton administration, is the Center's chief operating officer. The Center's fellows focus daily on hot-button issues in Washington, with an eye to influencing Congress, the public, and the media through sophisticated "rapid response" media campaigns run by Debbie Berger, the daughter of former Clinton national security adviser Samuel Berger.

Of course, this Center could also serve as another soft-money repository where the best policy minds in the Democratic Party could plan the embryonic stages of Hillary's presidential race and work up the policies of the next Clinton administration. Podesta told Jim VandeHei of the *Washington Post*, "She's strongly encouraging people, including myself, to get our act together, get out there, generate more ideas [and] market our ideas better."[11] Hillary's right-hand woman at HILLPAC, Patti Solis Doyle, told VandeHei that Hillary is "extremely supportive of the [groups] that Podesta and others are working on."

The Center will emulate Hillary's combative style. Partisan Democrats view the centrist Democratic Leadership Council's Progressive Policy Institute as almost Republican. The Brookings Institution, though well funded, is largely seen as an ineffectual collection of bow ties. The Institute for Policy Studies, though ideologically pure, is too much a caricature of Che-loving, Sandino-coffee-bean-picking leftists to be effective in Washington. The disparity between these groups and the clout of the conservative think tanks has obviously been worrying Hillary for some time. "The Republican Party in the United States had been masterful at creating a groundswell for conservative ideas after Senator Barry Goldwater's resounding defeat by Lyndon B. Johnson in the 1964 Presidential election," Hillary wrote in *Living History*. "Shocked by the margin of their party's losses, several Republican multimillionaires embarked on a strategy to seed conservative, even right-wing political philosophy, and to develop and advance specific policies to further it. They funded think tanks, endowed professorships and seminars and developed media channels for communicating ideas and opinions."[12]

Hillary is not just present at the creation of a new effort to combat the conservatives' war of ideas. She is likely its driving force—witness the promise of "rapid response" in the Center's charter, a tactic reminiscent of Hillary's aggressive, war-room style. So, too, can her hand be found in the creation of the American Constitution Society for Law and Policy, founded by the Clinton administration's acting solicitor general, Walter Dellinger, as a counterpart to the conservative Federalist Society. The Federalist Society was founded in part to counter the near-monolithic grip of liberals on the American Bar Association. But, of course, the liberalism of the ABA is insufficiently combative for Hillary, and so she now has the American Constitution Society for Law and Policy. Its recent national convention, the group's website advertised, brought Hillary into discourse on the state of the law with former attorney general Janet Reno, Ralph Neas, and that champion of the rule of law—at least Marxist law—Dr. Angela Davis. Dr. Davis has been a member of both the Black Panther Party and the Communist Party, and perhaps still is out of a reverence for things past.

It is possibly a manifestation of Hillary's paranoid mind, but she and many others on the left are also concerned with what they call right-wing control of the media, and she plans to do something about it. The left is obsessed in particular with Rush Limbaugh. They see Limbaugh's audience of twenty million as a free-floating mob capable of undoing all their good works in a moment's notice. All it takes is the right word from Rush behind the mike. Hillary's inordinate fear of Limbaugh spills over into a paranoia that at times seems clinical. She and her supporters see the FOX News Channel in a similarly hysterical light, and they are baffled as to why former New York governor Mario Cuomo, one of their legendary orators, and Jim Hightower, a political punster, failed to develop a mass audience. Phil Donahue's failure on cable news is another source of surprise.

Hillary's response to the left's failures in media is similar to her response to the left's failure in the war of ideas. She has excogitated a complicated theory best expressed by Al Gore when he theorized, "Something will start at the Republican National Committee, inside the building, and it will explode the next day on the right-wing talk show network and on FOX News and in the newspapers that play this game." He continued, "The FOX News network, the *Washington Times*, Rush Limbaugh—there's a bunch of them, and some of them are financed by wealthy, ultra-conservative billionaires who made political deals with Republican administrations and the rest of the media. . . . Most of the media [have] been slow to recognize the pervasive influence of this fifth column in their ranks." Yes, Gore actually calls people who disagree with him "fifth columnists."

The reason, of course, for the popularity of conservative commentators is that millions of Americans feel that they already get the liberal spin from the mainstream media. Conservative talk radio (and now, television) thrives because people are hungry for alternate viewpoints rarely found on the editorial pages of the *New York Times*. Not willing to concede, Hillary met with her Senate minority leader, Tom Daschle; Senator Jon Corzine of New Jersey; and North Dakota's Byron Dorgan, the chairman of the Democratic Policy Committee, to jump-start the effort to create a liberal media response.[13] "I know for a fact that Rob Reiner is talking with Michael Moore about helping with his 9/11 tape," a Hollywood insider says. He is referring to the effort to produce a film that would purport to link the Bush family, through George H. W. Bush's involvement with the high-finance Carlyle Group, to the family of Osama bin Laden.

Chicago venture capitalists Sheldon and Anita Drobny, certified Friends of Hillary, are doing their part by providing $10 million to launch AnShell Media, which will include a liberal radio talk network. The Drobnys hope to eventually raise $200 million. Clinton court jester Al Franken is sure to be a prominent host. So might Al Gore, who is also looking at lining up financing for a liberal cable television network, VTV, with Joel Hyatt (the same Hyatt who made a fortune by giving America the low-cost, strip mall trial lawyer).

Such efforts may not become commercial successes on the order of Limbaugh, Sean Hannity, or the *O'Reilly Factor*. But they will reach influential and impressionable audiences, and likely stay afloat through the largesse of liberal donors incensed by what they hear on the airwaves. In any event, all the talk of "right-wing radio" and FOX News serves another key purpose for Hillary. It helps discount anything they say about her when she finally runs for national office. Just as Hillary successfully sold the notion of a Vast Right-Wing Conspiracy on a morning television show, so, too, is she selling the traditional media on the notion that the growing influence of conservative media is, somehow, insidiously undermining a free press and, by extension, free elections—maybe even democracy itself. And they are buying. As a result of hand-wringing stories planted by liberals, notes Chriss Winston, a longtime Republican strategist and former deputy director for communications in the first Bush White House, "Suddenly, everyone is asking, 'Do conservative commentators have too much influence? Is FOX a threat to serious journalism?' We see angst-ridden reporters, editors, anchors, and producers from Washington to New York fearing mightily for the integrity of their profession and giving almost instant credibility to the Democrats' complaint of undue influence of conservative media.

"It isn't a tough sell to convince mainstream media types that influential conservative commentators and journalists are unfairly tipping the political scales," Winston says. "For most of them, who are already sympathetic to Democrat views, buying into the 'vast right-wing *media* conspiracy' is a little like a junk diet. Thanks to Hillary's clever absolution, tilting coverage to the left is now guilt-free. After all, in the world in which traditional journalists operate, they're just being fair."

The Plan

In the middle of the last century, a freshman United States senator named Lyndon Baines Johnson amassed stupendous power from inside the institution. He did it by identifying the vulnerabilities of powerful senators, shoring them up with corporate cash, and currying favor. Hillary Rodham Clinton has far surpassed Johnson, utterly taking over the Senate Democrats and the party itself—inside and out—and she has done it in a mere two years.

Now the Clintons have their network in place. They have their surrogates overseeing the money being raised for the official and unofficial organs of the Democratic Party. They have the issues campaigns of America Votes. They have the get-out-the-vote efforts of Americans Coming Together. They have the policy and propaganda shop at the Center for American Progress. And they have the megaphone of AnShell Media and perhaps Gore TV (though some things should be considered too lurid, even for cable).

Each of these parts is impressive. Together, these elements reinforce each other, forming the most formidable power base in Washington after that of Bush & Co. Hillary's position in the Senate leadership gives her the ability to set the legislative agendas that please powerful ideological lobbies, while HILLPAC allows her to drive those policies fueled by hard-money donations. The think tank provides policy guidance—and perhaps a highly articulated agenda for her presidency—while the new liberal media echoes and reinforces her ideas.

David Maraniss reports in his biography of the Clintons, *First in His Class*, that in 1973, "[w]hen Clinton told Diane Kincaid, the political science professor at Arkansas, how much she reminded him of Rodham and made him miss her, the professor asked him why he did not just marry Rodham and bring her to Arkansas. 'Because she's so good at what she does, she could have an amazing political career of her own,' Clinton said. 'If she comes to Arkansas it's going to be my state, my future. She could be president someday. She could go into any state and be elected to the Senate.'"[14]

Now it is her turn. Like a chess master, Hillary has moved her pawns and knights in a bold opening gambit. Are there any reasons to believe she will not go all the way?

CHAPTER TWO

The Day Job

"Compromise is another word that carries shades of weakness, vacillation, betrayal of ideals, surrender of moral principles. In the old culture, when virginity was a virtue, one referred to a woman's being 'compromised.' The word is generally regarded as ethically unsavory and ugly.

"But to the organizer, compromise is a key and beautiful word. It is always present in the pragmatics of operation. It is making the deal, getting that vital breather, usually the victory. If you start with nothing, demand 100 percent, then compromise for 30 percent, you're 30 percent ahead."[1]

—*Saul Alinsky*

IN GENERATIONS PAST, THERE HAVE BEEN other Ivy Leaguers, all male, who by dint of intelligence, hard work, and canny politicking found themselves poised for a presidential campaign: Roosevelts, Kennedys, Tafts. But today a woman can play this epic role. She marries well, expanding her influence through a husband who wields enormous power. She heads important organizations in her own right. Then she makes her run for the White House.

Such a woman, of course, could be Elizabeth Dole of North Carolina.

"If anything, Elizabeth is much more impressive than Hillary," says
a top Senate aide. "Dole held two Cabinet jobs, ran a humanitarian
organization with a multi-billion budget, also had the 'native daughter' issue—though she had grown up in North Carolina and had been
educated at Duke before going off to Harvard Law and Washington."

Hillary herself notes Dole's poise and intelligence, adding, "It's a
strange twist of fate that we now both serve in the Senate."[2]

But for all of Dole's competence and résumé building, she was a
disaster in her 2000 race for the presidency. There have been thirty-
three women senators; at present, fourteen senators are women. None
of them save Hillary Rodham Clinton is a credible presidential aspi-
rant. Only Hillary has the stature, the following, and the stage presence to go all the way.

To get from the Senate Democratic cloakroom to the Oval Office,
however, Hillary has to first prove herself as an able legislator. She
must prove herself to be something more than a celebrity elected as a
fluke. "I'm working harder than I ever have in my life," her Senate colleagues report her as telling them. In the White House, she had the
ability to regulate her schedule. A senator's day is totally controlled by
an inflexible schedule of floor votes, incessant morning and evening
fund-raisers, and interminable "town hall meetings" in distinctly
unglamorous towns.

Perhaps Hillary's hardest task, however, is not keeping up with the
demands of the job. It is keeping Madame Hillary under wraps. It has
not been easy for Hillary to be a good senator, for the Senate makes
demands that are contrary to her nature. The rules of the Senate allow
any member to effectively blackball the initiatives of any other

member. This enforces collegiality, bipartisanship, and good-natured compromise—hardly the qualities associated with Hillary's combative political style.

She is, after all, a born autocrat, not a born compromiser.

As first lady and health care reformer, Hillary raised suspicions in Congress by developing an absurdly complex health care policy in secret meetings, then further offended the *exaltés* of the Hill with her patronizing drop-bys. In 1994, the comment of a Washington insider to the *New Yorker* typified the Hill's reaction to Hillary: "She is so thin-skinned; she really believes that if you criticize one page of a 1,364-page bill you're the enemy."[3]

As a newly elected senator, she heightened fears with a few greenhorn mistakes. The most public of these was her theatrical discomfort during President George W. Bush's address to a joint session of Congress following the September 11, 2001, terrorist attacks. "She grimaced," observed columnist Michelle Malkin. "She sighed. She rolled her eyes. She fidgeted like a five-year-old at an opera. And when Mrs. Clinton mustered enough energy to clap, she acted as if there were razor blades strapped to her palms."[4] The cameras had caught Hillary unaware, showing a vestige of the woman the late Michael Kelly had excoriated on her road to the Senate as a "carpetbagger nonpareil; she has never held elective office; she made a ham-fisted mess of her one formal attempt to craft national policy, the 1993 health care reform; she appears to regard power, in her case, as something approaching a divine right; she epitomizes the scorched-earth politics that have already crippled the ability of Congress and the White House to make law."[5] Kelly also noted, tellingly, that "while Clinton is brilliant at performance politics, Gore is barely competent; Hillary is flatly incompetent."[6] When she arrived in the Senate, her colleagues feared her.

One senator says he was worried when he first saw Senator Clinton striding away from the Senate floor with a "gaggle" of young women in tow. "They looked like groupies following a rock star," he says with a notable edge of disgust.

A senior GOP aide says, "She had a celebrity aura that made members wary of her. Senators were very worried about intrusiveness of the Secret Service. Republicans were not sure how to deal with her." Then he adds what dozens of other Senate insiders now corroborate, namely, that Hillary seemed to undergo an overnight transformation. She figured out that to become president, she first had to become a good senator; to be a good senator, the Hillary of health care, angry outbursts, and airborne ashtrays had to be submerged.

"Once she was here, Hillary was especially diligent in breaking through the partisan persona," one insider says. "She looked for opportunities to co-sponsor [legislation] with Republicans on just about anything."

One senator recalls, "There were a few incidents early on with the Secret Service. But they learned how to fit in, and the Senate learned how to accommodate them. Hillary has done this [the transition from first lady to senator] shrewdly. She was very smart in handling herself. She could have made big news just in her floor speeches; instead, she was low-key, reassuring to colleagues."

A Republican lobbyist with no love for Hillary nevertheless winds up praising her for forgoing the Senate subway and walking the long tunnel connecting the Capitol with the Senate offices, lest her entourage of security and aides crowd other senators and visitors out of a ride. A Capitol policewoman assigned to Hillary was initially concerned about the press reports of the former first lady as an abusive harridan, according to one insider, "but when she worked for her she liked her."

Hillary is performing many other unnatural acts of fellowship. It is hard to imagine a deeper generational gulf than the one between Hillary Rodham Clinton and Robert C. Byrd of West Virginia, reformed segregationist, self-styled "dean" of the Senate, an octogenarian who holds himself spellbound in the conviction that he is a Ciceronian orator. Yet Hillary took pains to pay a respectful visit to Byrd to solicit his advice about how to be a senator.[7]

Having curtsied before Byrd, Hillary proceeded to prove to the Republicans that she was a player. She co-signed legislation on foster children with one-time impeachment leader Tom DeLay—whom she describes in her autobiography, *Living History*, in words that sound as if they were spoken through gritted teeth. DeLay, she writes, is "perhaps the most partisan and effective leader of the extreme conservatives in the House."[8] Even when trying to be gracious, however, there is always the dig—note the sobriquet "extreme."

A Republican aide says that when Hillary gets in a committee meeting with Republican colleagues, "they talk like friends, they whisper, they could be talking about legislation, they could be talking about last night's baseball game, they talk like buddies." A female lobbyist sees gender at work. "You know how it is when men and women work together. Even though everything's aboveboard, there's always a subtle undercurrent of, well, flirting. Hillary does that, she flirts well."

In the summer of 2003, Hillary reemerged as a national figure with her stinging denunciations of President Bush and her global book tour for *Living History*. Before she could reemerge as a potential president, however, she first had to be an earnest student of the Senate's arcane rules and knotty issues.

Before she could schmooze on television with Barbara and Katie, she first had to win the Golden Gavel award for presiding over the Senate for more than one hundred hours in one year.

Before she could safely seek global best-sellerdom via her memoir, with its tales of grievance and intrigue, Hillary first had to generate headlines such as this one in the *Syracuse Post-Standard*: "Smart Schools Save Energy," and this in the *Daily Star* of Oneonta: "Small Farms Can't Be Forgotten."

Before she could become the nation's watchdog for homeland security, Hillary had to first wade into local politics. The same woman who warned us of the Vast Right-Wing Conspiracy is now telling us, "New York is the third-largest producer of tart cherries in the nation, and a significant producer of sweet cherries."[9] Moreover, Hillary has shown an appreciation of the thing most essential for being a successful senator—a good staff. Says one long-time Friend of Bill, "She's done a great job locking up good folks."

The praise for her staff is near universal—a break from her earlier record. "There were a lot of early tensions in her office," says a Republican Senate aide. "Hillary set out to push her New York agenda, but a lot of her staff was from the White House. Her staff's agenda was more national than hers. She knew this wasn't what she needed. She knew she hadn't clinched the deal with upstate New York. She had won only because she ran against a pathetic Republican candidate who had virtually ignored upstate."

After a period of turnover, Hillary finally wound up with a staff that political analyst Charlie Cook calls "world class."[10] "Don't you think she's exceptionally well prepared whenever she goes out onto the floor?" says one Democratic operative close to minority leader Tom Daschle. "She's done her homework."

Of course, such comments often have a man-bites-dog quality to them. Can you believe it? Hillary displaying discipline and actually being nice? As hard as she tries, though, Madame Hillary still shows through the patina of a new professionalism.

"It was unfortunate, I thought we had an agreement," said Senate budget chairman Don Nickles, knife freshly planted in his back. Like other Republicans, he had been eager to demonstrate his bipartisanship. He co-sponsored legislation with Hillary, in this instance an extension of jobless benefits—only to find that Hillary upended the deal with a surprise amendment. More important, to her, than bipartisanship was rolling Senate majority leader Bill Frist on his first day as manager of the Senate floor.[11] Hillary's betrayal succeeded. She forced Frist, a novice at grand parliamentary maneuver, to agree to consider expanding the program in a future debate.

Frist got another taste of Hillary's prehensile nature when he and Senator Larry Craig of Idaho set up a press conference with actor Bruce Willis in June 2003, to heighten awareness of the plight of children in foster care. A press release soon appeared from Hillary's office, giving the Senate majority leader second billing at his own event. Senate aides were agog to see Hillary elbow her way to the forefront of the Willis appearance. "Bruce Willis wasn't pleased to see her there," one observer says. "You could tell he didn't like her one bit."

Another apparent recipient of the Hillary treatment is fellow Democrat Mary Landrieu of Louisiana. In late 2002, Landrieu was on the ropes in her attempt to win reelection, under fierce attack by Republican challenger Suzanne Haik Terrell, who was riding high on a cool million dollars in campaign funds raised for her by President George W. Bush in the last week of the campaign. Worst of all for Landrieu, the young senator had alienated her African-American base, the key to victory for any Southern Democrat. In order to keep more conservative white Democrats in line, Landrieu had stressed how often she had voted for Bush administration goals. This helped attract suburban whites, but at the price of alienating urban black voters.

At her most vulnerable moment, Landrieu's *deus ex machina* descended in the form of Bill Clinton, who used his unique standing in the African-American community to make phone calls that galvanized church leaders. Landrieu squeaked into reelection with 41,000 votes. In New Orleans, where 63 percent of registered voters are black, Landrieu's margin of victory was a decisive 4 to 1.[12]

What happened next baffled some observers of the Armed Services Committee. Landrieu was in the middle ranks of the committee, clearly ready to inherit the committee staff and clout that comes with a major subcommittee designation. One Republican defense intellectual close to the committee says he was surprised that Landrieu quit the committee when she did. He says she "wasn't up for the normal committee rotation, and Louisiana is such a big shipbuilding state—Armed Services is such a natural fit."

"In Louisiana, the Army's got Fort Polk, the Air Force has got Barksdale," a Republican observer of the committee says. "For a Democrat to be successful in Louisiana, she has to be seen doing something for the boys and girls in blue and green. Landrieu was not happy about it."

A Democrat close to the Senate Armed Services Committee offers an explanation. He says that as soon as Landrieu arrived back in Washington, she was surprised—and upset—to learn that there was a price attached to her salvation by the Clintons. She was told in no uncertain terms that she had to quit Armed Services in order to relinquish a spot for Hillary. Landrieu acquiesced to the change, clearing the way for Hillary to burnish her national security credentials.

Landrieu's office dismisses this scenario as "nonsense," saying that Senate rules required her to simplify her two "Super A" committee assignments. (Before losing her position on Armed Services, the senator had obtained a waiver to serve on both Armed Services and her other Super A appointment, Appropriations.) Had Landrieu stayed on Armed Services, however, she would have risen in rank on the committee. She is now the least-ranking member on the agriculture subcommittee and the least-ranking member on the subcommittee that oversees health and human services. She was not appointed to the defense subcommittee, where she could have transferred some of her Armed Services interests. Nor was she appointed to the media-intense subcommittee on homeland defense. Incredibly, for a Louisianan, she was not appointed to the critical energy and water subcommittee. She was made the least-ranking member on military construction—a subcommittee headed by Kay Bailey Hutchinson, a conservative Republican from a neighboring state often in competition with Louisiana for military appropriations.

"They threw her military operations as a sop, and boy is she miserable and unhappy," says a Democratic insider close to the Armed Services Committee.

Worst of all, Landrieu became the least-ranking member of the foreign operations subcommittee, an appointment that in her next race will force her to explain to Louisiana taxpayers why the United States gives away billions of dollars to Iraq and other foreign countries.

A Republican veteran of Armed Services says, "If Landrieu had stayed on Armed Services, she would have been ranking on something important, she would have had a lot of chances to stand under the clock," referring to the alcove under a large clock in the Capitol where senators routinely give interviews for television news. "The bottom line is that Hillary made Landrieu pay a price in terms of media exposure and real power."

There are other signs that Madame Hillary, though subdued, is far from vanquished.

When one senatorial colleague is asked about Hillary's charm, he shouts, "No! She stares at you across the table, those eyes cold, calculating. She holds a grudge. She looks like she has ice water in her veins. On our first meeting, I welcomed her and said hello. She's got this kind of frozen smile, but her eyes beam another message. She says nice things, but you get the sense that she hates you."

The senator is not through.

"She will work with you just fine, but if she sees you as an enemy, or as partisan or as right wing, there is no charm, no camaraderie. Oh, she started off by saying hello to Strom Thurmond, and making nice with Jesse Helms. But the only Republicans she really has any use for are the really liberal ones like Susan Collins or Lincoln Chafee. Her every action betrays a deep-seated hatred of conservatism."

Another senator says, "She's more disciplined than in the White House, and more poisonously partisan than Bill."

A Republican aide agrees. "Underneath it all, I believe she regards anyone who disagrees with her as an enemy and a fool."

Steering the Senate

"Clearly, she understands the mechanisms of influence," says one Senate staffer. "She has demonstrated an extraordinary ability to establish herself within the Democratic caucus." In early January 2003, Robert Novak reported that Hillary worked behind the scenes to calm a rebellion against Senate Democratic leader Tom Daschle by Richard Durbin of Illinois.[13]

Invisible to the public, Hillary has risen into one of the most powerful jobs in the Senate Democratic leadership. It did not take her long to locate the Senate sweet spot in the form of the Steering and Coordination Committee, the place where the wish lists of big money, liberal interest groups (labor, trial lawyers, enviros, and far-out lobbies like NOW and People for the American Way) get a say on the Democrats' internal policy agenda.

The appointment so rankled Chuck Schumer, her nominal senior, that Senate Democratic leader Tom Daschle had to appease him with the special (read: minor) leadership post of "regional whip." (Putting two senators from the same state in the leadership is highly unusual, a move that perturbs senators in both parties.)

Her position on the Steering Committee also puts her in charge of a taxpayer-funded entity that exists solely for partisan agenda-setting and political agitprop. The Republicans have a much more loosely organized caucus organized around seniority, not party discipline. This gives Republicans more freedom to defy their caucus, a fact that has often brought grief to Republican presidents. (The GOP's rough counterpart to the Democrats' Steering Committee is the more loosely organized Senate Republican Conference Committee. The more conservative members of the Republican caucus operate a small, informal Steering Committee of their own.)

"There are some people inside the caucus grumbling, suggesting she wants to bring more of a war-room mentality to the Senate than some senators are comfortable with," a top Senate Democratic aide told James VandeHei of the *Washington Post*. "Others think this also has to be viewed with her future presidential runs and national ambitions in mind."[14]

Why do Democrats put up with her and the impositions she inflicts on them? The diagnosis of one Republican senator: "When she started raising money, well, big money calms a lot of people." Another senator adds: "Daschle doesn't want a public spat with her, so he bows to her confrontational tactics."

Unlike Schumer's token assignment, there is nothing minor about Hillary's position, which gives her a powerful lash in having a say on the approval of committee assignments. Cross her and you might not get that coveted post.

That power of hers undoubtedly assuages a lot of otherwise uneasy *exaltés* as well.

Arming for War

Some future Robert Caro, Lyndon Johnson's embarrassingly thorough biographer, will have plenty of illuminating material in chronicling Hillary's freshman rise to the front ranks of the Senate minority leadership. No act, however, does more to illuminate Hillary's presidential aspirations than her lunge for a spot on the Armed Services Committee. Hillary is the first New Yorker to be appointed to the committee since it was formed in 1947.

"Hillary makes Bobby Fischer moves," says Philip Kawior, a Republican political consultant based in Illinois. "It's only ten moves later that you begin to see the strategy unfold." Armed Services has been her most counterintuitive move in the Senate. Visiting upstate New York's Fort Drum with President Bush to personally thank the 10th Mountain Division for its service in Afghanistan is hardly what one expects of someone schooled on the ramparts of the anti-war movement. It is less incongruous when you remember that as a young woman who had just moved to Arkansas to begin her partnership with Bill—fresh from her radical days at Yale Law and work as a House impeachment attorney against President Richard M. Nixon—Hillary had tried to join the U.S. Marine Corps, a killer political credential for a woman in the era of so-called Chicken Hawk men. (This alone is proof, if it was ever needed, that the young Hillary who wrote to NASA to inquire about becoming an astronaut had her heart set early on another sky-high dream, the presidency.)

"New York and Armed Services—it's not a natural fit," says a prominent former Pentagon official who frequently deals with the committee. "In Virginia, you worry about Norfolk and sea power. In Georgia, you worry about the F-22 and C-130s. But it's a good combination—to be engaged in homeland security and national security. Take those together and she's got a good basis for some of the claims she wants to make as a national candidate."

Hillary steers clear of the classic liberal agenda on defense—arms control test bans and opposition to missile defense. From a quiet, effective committee drudge, Hillary has emerged as the Democratic Party's most persistent critic of President Bush, especially on homeland security. "Bill Clinton doesn't address the issues in the same tone," says Kawior. "Hillary's more genuine, she is the true believer. She gathers in all the acolytes. She's the best since Bobby Kennedy to capture the rhetorical essence of the Democratic Party. None of the presidential candidates can come close."

However, it would be a mistake to see Hillary's attacks on the Bush administration as logically planned thrusts in a strategic attack. Her radical ideological mentor Saul Alinsky preached, as we shall see, that an organizer had to be an opportunist who worked off instinct. Alinsky believed that reality was too complex, too shifting, to work off a hard and fast plan—one has to go by feel.

Hillary rarely lets an opportunity slide by. The rubble was still smoking in the pit of the ruined World Trade Center site when Hillary held up a *New York Post* headline saying, "Bush Knew." Hillary added,

"The president knew what?" Like conservatives who once espoused the belief that FDR knew the Japanese would attack Pearl Harbor, immediately following the September 11 attacks Hillary intimated that the president had known what was coming—and was now engaged in a coverup.

It may have delighted her to display the usually conservative *Post* running a headline condemning President Bush. But her attack put her in the company of Congresswoman Cynthia McKinney, conspiracy theorist and left-wing scourge of Israel. Hillary, however, was too smart to linger on this point. Congresswoman McKinney did, and was soon tossed out of office by Georgia voters. Hillary received an instant embrace from her party's hard left and moved on. When House minority leader Nancy Pelosi of California said she was "devastated by the fact that we are going to war," Hillary remained mum.[15]

When Daschle heaped more blame on President Bush than on Saddam Hussein—"I'm saddened, saddened that this president failed so miserably at diplomacy that we're now forced to war"—Hillary did not play follow the leader.[16] When Congressman Jim McDermott went to Baghdad at the eve of the war to call Bush a liar, Hillary stayed home.

In fact, Hillary ultimately voted for the resolution empowering President Bush to wage the war, but she did so with a perfect equipoise. She managed to sound vehemently anti-Saddam without sounding pro-Bush. A Senate colleague explains, "She does not want to do anything that will help Bush." Hillary, the Coat and Tie Radical of the late 1960s—the radical who attempts to subvert "the system" from within—maintains an especial rivalry for her generational opposites, the conservatives who seek nothing more than to preserve the constitution and the American way of life.

In a floor speech on the measure to authorize the use of force against Iraq, Hillary managed quite a juggling act, keeping a whole cupboard full of teacups and saucers spinning in the air. She criticized the United Nations for putting limits on inspection sites. She warned of Saddam Hussein's ambitions for weapons of mass destruction: "It is clear, however, that if left unchecked, Saddam Hussein will continue to increase his capacity to wage biological and chemical warfare, and will keep trying to develop nuclear weapons." She worried that an unchecked Saddam could endanger the entire Middle East (read: Israel). She fretted that a "unilateral" attack could prompt Russia to attack Chechen rebels in Georgia, China to attack Taiwan, and India to attack Pakistan. She concluded that going to war against Iraq "on the present facts is not a good option"—but voted to enable George W. Bush to lead the nation into war.

For good measure, at other times she warned that attacking Saddam Hussein would encourage attacks on the United States. Yet she also found Secretary of State Colin Powell's presentation to the United Nations to be "compelling."[17] The redoubtable Deborah Orin of the *New York Post* led the press in chronicling the mutations of Hillary's Iraq policy, from Hillary's saying that she didn't agree "100 percent" with the president's approach, to saying that she "fully supports" him.[18] Hillary told *Meet the Press* that the president's policy "is exactly what should be done."[19] Finally, in a little grace note, Hillary reminded reporters that Vice President Dick Cheney once said that wars were won with the military bequeathed by previous administrations. If Cheney wanted to write a letter of thanks to Bill Clinton, "I'd be happy to deliver it personally."[20]

Her gyrations prompted one Senate official to comment that "Hillary is at war with herself." Nevertheless, her highly nuanced support for Operation Iraqi Freedom achieved its goal of putting her in the mainstream of nationally electable Democrats. Hillary must have been delighted when *Weekly Standard* editor William Kristol lumped her with the patriotic "Dick Gephardt" liberals against "the Dominique de Villepin" left. Kristol went on to group Hillary in the tradition of the Harry Truman wing of the Democratic Party, as opposed to the Henry Wallace/George McGovern wing.[21] Kristol's analysis is not off base. Hillary's vote did isolate her from the fringes of the anti-war movement populated by the likes of McKinney and McDermott.

In her senatorial campaign Hillary managed a similar reinvention. She went from kissing Suha Arafat, after Mrs. Arafat had peddled vicious lies about Israel gassing Palestinian women and children, to being a stout defender of Israeli civilians in the face of Arafat's aggression—"it becomes clear that these very determined adversaries are absolutely committed . . . to the destruction of Israel." Likewise, she now emerges from the September 11 environment free from radical taint. Like the old cigarette jingle "You've come a long way, baby!" Hillary has made immense strides toward setting herself up as a credible commander-in-chief. And she did not have to go to boot camp to do it.

Homeland Offense

Every two years, former governors, military officers, and corporate executives arrive at the Capitol as newly elected senators—only to be disappointed. Executive leaders who are accustomed to motivating people, challenging organizations, and producing hard-and-fast results often find the job of senator—for all its demands—a tiresome debating society.

Not Hillary. For her the Senate is a stage on which to daily engage in the street theater and agitprop of the professional radical. She holds to another tenet of her radical mentor Alinsky: Though the activist knows that compromise is inevitable, while an issue is in play it is necessary to portray that issue in the most polarizing terms possible. Writing to the activists of Hillary's youth, Alinsky noted, "Our cause had to be all shining justice, allied with the angels; theirs had to be all evil, tied to the Devil; in no war has the enemy or the cause ever been gray."[22]

This was a message that Hillary, as co-president pushing nationalized health care, took too literally. Hillary has since internalized the rest of the Alinsky formula, that the next step after polarization is compromise and resolution—taking the thirty percent you can get.

Now the new Hillary daily enacts Alinsky's prescriptions on the Senate floor, but in a more nuanced way, mixing the sweet with the sour. She followed his game plan magnificently in taking on Republican leader Frist. First, Hillary went on the attack, undermining a solemn agreement made with the Republicans on the extension of unemployment insurance, only to eventually relent and settle for an agreement to revisit the expansion of one of her beloved programs. Again, recall Alinsky, who wrote, "What I am saying is that the organizer must be able to split himself into two parts—one part in the arena of action where he polarizes the issue to 100 to nothing, and helps to lead his forces into conflict, while the other part knows that when the time comes for negotiations that it really is only a 10 percent difference—and yet both parts have to live comfortably with each other."[23]

This formula explains why staid Senate Republicans have such a hard time understanding Hillary. How can she be so nice on the floor, and then turn around and say these awful things about us? They do not grasp the purpose of agitprop: To force a compromise in her direction, it is first necessary to disturb the peace.

The red meat speeches for the party faithful now occupy a central place on Hillary's rhetorical menu. At the top of her list is the contention that President George W. Bush somehow let down New York City and America on September 11, 2001. In some of her attacks, Hillary makes it seem as if Bush secretly wanted to see harm done to New York City. Consider how the senator belabored a report from EPA inspector general Nikki Tinsley, another holdover from the Clinton administration. Tinsley's report accused the White House of exerting political pressure to keep New Yorkers unaware of the danger of particulate pollution in the aftermath of the collapse of the World Trade Center. Former New York mayor Rudy Giuliani told Matt Lauer of the *Today Show* that Tinsley's report was "not consistent with all the other reports we had." To be outraged over this, one would have to ignore the fact that the EPA's original assessment was that particulate pollution was not a problem, and that that original assessment squared with what state, local, and other environmental agencies found. One would also have to discount the confusion and panic that followed the attack, as well as the unsettled state of science on human health and toxicity.

Senator Clinton declared, "I know a little bit about how White Houses work. I know somebody picked up the phone, somebody got on a computer, somebody sent an email, somebody called for a meeting, somebody in that White House probably under instructions from somebody further up the chain told the EPA, 'Don't tell the people of New York the truth.'" She concluded, "I want to know who that is."[24]

This explanation likely reveals more about how things worked in the Clinton White House than in the White House of George W. Bush.

In short, Hillary would have us believe that for some reason the Bush administration wants New Yorkers to breathe bad air; but the worst form of air pollution in New York is undoubtedly the *Kultursmog* emitted by Madame Hillary and her fellow leftists, poisoning the cultural air with such absurd attacks. As with the rest of the American left, Hillary's fundamental political value remains to disturb the peace, which, incidentally, is a misdemeanor.

Pursuant to disturbing the peace, one of Hillary's favorite tactics is to demand an explanation, no matter how silly the charge. Hillary demanded a White House explanation of what the President knew before September 11, 2001, as she held that copy of the "Bush Knew" issue of the *New York Post* in her hand. She demanded an explanation over the EPA report. By late summer 2003, when she demanded an explanation in the midst of the blackout in the Northeast, Hillary's trick had lost its novelty. She even met with widespread ridicule—as if all the governors, members of Congress, Department of Energy officials, and electric utility executives would fail to seek an explanation for the power grid crash without Senator Clinton to prod this question along.

Still, she will risk a little embarrassment for the opportunity to cause controversy. The EPA report, the blackouts, all are issues of momentary political opportunity for the junior senator from New York. Hillary's highest hopes remain centered on embarrassing the Bush administration on homeland security. While doing her share of grant announcements ("Senator Clinton announces $4 million for gas masks for the New York Police Department"), Hillary is always ready to up the ante. No matter how much the Bush administration does on homeland security, it will never be enough. She will always accuse it of doing too little, too late. (Never mind that the same polemical lens could be focused on her. For weeks Hillary and her fellow Democrats delayed the creation of a Homeland Security Department in order to protect government union featherbedding.)

To be sure, constructive criticism is a patriotic duty when it comes to homeland security. Hillary is more interested in scoring political points—and in setting the political predicate for her bid for national office. Say what one will about the Bush administration's approach to safeguarding America; whatever its deficiencies, it does not lack a sense of urgency or a will to defend the country. Nevertheless, in Hillary's rhetoric, the Bush administration is sleeping as soundly as a sailor dozing in the hold of the USS *Arizona* on the morning of December 7, 1941.

"We have relied on a myth of homeland security—a myth written in rhetoric, inadequate resources, and a new bureaucracy, instead of relying on good, old-fashioned American ingenuity, might, and muscle," she says.[25]

What would constitute a good, old-fashioned American solution to the danger of a chemical, nuclear, or biological attack? Hillary's solution is disingenuous—and clever.

A document from her office explains that the senator "introduced the Homeland Security Block Grant Act, which provides that 70 percent of homeland security funding should go directly to more than 1,000 cities and counties across the United States. The remaining 30 percent will be sent to the States, which will serve as a pass-through directed to smaller communities."

Thus the bulk of homeland security spending would go to local funding for police, fire, and other local first providers in homeland defense.

Never mind how likely it is that any amount of funding for the firefighters of Genesee County could prevent a major terror attack. Never mind that much of this spending would go toward items traditionally labeled as "pork." That is not the point. The point is the likelihood that well before 2008, something terrible will once again happen in America—and then Hillary Clinton will be able to say, *I told you so*. In the aftermath of an attack, Hillary Clinton will have positioned herself to stand before the nation and demand yet another explanation from the Bush White House. She will also be, by implication, the woman with the plan.

Parliamentary Piracy

"In the entire history of the U.S. Senate, the filibuster was kept away from judicial nominations—until now," one Republican Senate aide says. "Who do you think thought up that one?"

Far from being a sacred Constitutional prerogative, the Senate filibuster has a troubled history (reflected, appropriately enough, in the derivation of the word from a Dutch word for "pirate"). The filibuster arose in the nineteenth century out of respect for the senatorial right of unlimited debate. It soon devolved into a mechanism for minorities to thwart the democratic process. It has most recently morphed into the Democrats' favorite means for making judicial nominees walk the plank.

Concern over the nature of the filibuster led to its being curtailed somewhat in 1917, when Rule 22 allowed a two-thirds majority (sixty-six votes out of the Senate's one hundred—reduced in 1975 to sixty votes) to invoke "cloture"—that is, to end debate and allow an up-or-down vote in which the majority wins. Over the years, the filibuster has been romanticized, from chuckling over Senator Huey Long's late-night readings of endless recipes for "potlikker" and fried oysters, to the near-legendary status of Strom Thurmond's famous all-nighters, to the drama of Jimmy Stewart's rhetorical last stand in Frank Capra's film *Mr. Smith Goes to Washington.* The true history of the filibuster is less appealing. It was used in a futile effort to force the Senate to seat the corrupt racist Theodore Bilbo of Mississippi. The longest filibuster ever acted out on the Senate floor was exercised by Strom Thurmond of South Carolina, who tested the limits of the human bladder with a twenty-four hour, eighteen minute rant against the 1957 Civil Rights Act. A further monument to the filibuster was a fourteen hour, thirteen minute screed by the former Ku Klux Klan grand kleagle, Senator Robert C. Byrd of West Virginia. He was filibustering against the 1964 Civil Rights Act until cloture was ultimately invoked, and the historic measure passed with the support of minority leader Everett Dirksen and other Republicans.

Throughout the history of the filibuster, however, it has never been used against court appointments. (The power of the filibuster was invoked, but ultimately not needed, to stymie LBJ's nomination of U.S. Supreme Court associate justice Abe Fortas to be chief justice shortly before it became public that the justice was taking money on the side.) In the history of the Republic, says Senator John Cornyn, former Texas attorney general and member of the Judiciary Committee, "no judicial nomination has ever been stopped by filibuster—until now."[26]

"The attitude has always been that the president should get confirmation of the nominees of his choice," one senator explains. "It's not a matter of Senate rules, but of Senate tradition—you just don't filibuster judicial nominations."

That this Senate tradition changed with the arrival of Hillary Rodham Clinton is likely not a coincidence. As we shall see, in every position that she has ever held—from executive branch appointments to the unofficial office of first lady—Hillary Clinton has managed to undermine or radicalize every institution she has touched.

"The political handling of the judiciary, these harsh tactics, they're all Hillary traits," says a Republican senator. A senior aide close to the Senate leadership adds, "Clearly the more liberal wing of the Democratic caucus is in control," though he sees as much influence on the caucus coming from Ted Kennedy, the mastodon of paleo-liberalism.

Today, and for the first time, the Senate minority is regularly employing the filibuster to delay and derail a sitting president's nominations for appellate and district courts. The most public victim of this strategy was Miguel Estrada, a Honduran immigrant who graduated with honors from Columbia University and Harvard Law School, and who served as assistant solicitor general for five years under President Clinton before being nominated for the appellate bench by President Bush.

The excuse for blackballing Estrada was that he refused to produce confidential attorney-client memoranda that he wrote in the solicitor general's office in the Department of Justice. Every living former solicitor general—four Democrats, three Republicans—defended Estrada's refusal to release these confidential memoranda. Still, Hillary has remained voluble in opposition: "Time and again, this administration is proving itself to flout the rule of law, to be very concerned with secrecy, unwilling to share information with the elected representatives of the American people."[27] That about sums up independent counsel Ken Starr's complaint against the Clintons' treatment of his Whitewater subpoenas.

In a tartly worded letter to Senate Democrats, White House counsel Alberto Gonzales remonstrated that none of the seven prior judicial nominees who had worked in the solicitor general's office had been asked to produce these confidential documents, reminding the Democrats of the former solicitor generals' support for Estrada and concern that to demand his confidential documents was an assault on the independence of the office.

Senate sources say that while former New York colleague Chuck Schumer led the charge against Estrada, Hillary played a vital though largely behind-the-scenes role in bucking up the Democratic caucus and in organizing prominent, self-styled civil rights leaders to come to Washington to denounce the young nominee.

"She is behind a group that urges Daschle to obstruct judicial appointments," a Republican senator said. "She is the 'titular leader' of liberal Democrats in the Senate. In terms of strategy, she is given a good deal of respect by the liberals. She is terrified of making the president look good, so she tries to get fellow senators to obstruct."

The campaign to filibuster Estrada's nomination to the U.S. Circuit Court of Appeals lasted for two years, until the nominee, citing family issues, withdrew. "The change that has occurred in judicial nominations, this is totally unprecedented," says a Republican senator. The Democrats could care less that long years of Senate tradition—and bipartisanship—have been trashed. Or that the Senate ignored the intentions of Alexander Hamilton, who specified in *Federalist 76* that the Senate's advise and consent role was to prevent nepotism, corrupt appointments, and partisan grandstanding in the judiciary.

"The idea of prudence, fairness, the precedent she's setting for the nominations of a future Democratic president—all of this means nothing to her," the Republican senator says. "Harmony is not her objective. She is truly transforming the Senate."

Of course, that future Democratic president could well be Hillary herself.

"Dear Colleagues"

In her coming bid for the presidency, Hillary faces two possible pitfalls. To run in 2008, she will need to stand for Senate reelection in 2006. To achieve this, Hillary must quell the growing undercurrent of resentment among her Senate Democratic colleagues. The other potential pitfall is her cavalier coverage of New York issues, heavy on headlines, light on substance.

Hillary's colleagues in the Senate Democratic caucus are learning that Madame Hillary can be suppressed, but she can never be eliminated. Russ Feingold, the upright Wisconsin Democrat, discovered this shortly after joining with John McCain to sponsor a campaign finance reform bill. By the summer of 2002, Democratic strategists and politicians were becoming aware that the raft of new restrictions on spending attached to McCain-Feingold would make it difficult for their billionaire trial lawyers and labor bosses to invest large, soft-dollar donations in Democrats. At a closed-door meeting of Democratic senators, Hillary tallied up the damage done to Democratic campaigns by Feingold's legislation and then lit into him with a "live in the real world" tirade.

"She tore into Feingold," a Senate aide says. "Other people at the caucus were not happy about it. The other Democrats resent her. But they're so weak, their weakness permits her to grow." There is, of course, a subtext here, as there often is with Hillary's antics. Though Feingold ultimately voted to acquit William Jefferson Clinton during the 1999 impeachment trial, he did provide the only Democratic vote against a motion to dismiss the charges. In other words, Feingold supported the impeachment of President Clinton, though he ultimately opposed conviction.

"Hillary doesn't forget things like this," says one Senate observer.

Feingold, however, was mauled only once. Hillary's colleague, Chuck Schumer, must feel like a tiger trainer in a tight cage. Their relationship began on a good note. Hillary had made her first systematic tour of New York state politics in a campaign to pump up then–Representative Schumer in his effort to defeat Senator Al D'Amato, as well she should have. D'Amato had tormented the Clintons as chair of the Senate Whitewater Committee. The irony is that once elected, Schumer became more D'Amato than D'Amato. "Like D'Amato, Schumer's everywhere," says one national political correspondent who covered them both. "On bread and butter issues like ATM fees, D'Amato did all that stuff, Schumer's all over it."

A senator says, "I suppose there's no love lost between Hillary Clinton and Chuck Schumer. I'd be surprised if there wasn't quite a bit of tension. He is in a position where he can't verbalize—can't even acknowledge—how much she gets under his skin."

Around New York state, Schumer is known as "the Brooklyn farmer" for trekking to remote county fairs upstate, the kind of places where blue ribbons are awarded in the best pie contests or to the kid in Future Farmers of America who raised the most splendiferous hog. Inside the institution, Schumer has quite a different reputation. Some believe he is getting what he deserves in Hillary Clinton—that were it not for her celebrity, he would be stiffing her just as she stiffs him.

"No one likes to work with him, he's a liar and a grandstander," a Republican aide says. "I ended up recruiting her [Hillary] as a co-signer on a bill because she has to work with this jerk. Schumer tries to insert certain of his issues onto her issues. He insists everything is his issue."

The Republican then repeats a couple of old saws I used to hear applied to D'Amato: "He's often described as a senator who behaves as a House member. There's no more unsafe place to be than between Schumer and a TV camera. He has to hold weekly media briefings in New York in which he makes news by announcing grants or calls for something. It irks him no end that Hillary can make news just by being who she is."

Sometimes, this relationship gets physical.

"She has the sharpest elbows in town," says one New Yorker who watched Hillary in a duel of elbows with Chuck Schumer to get to the cameras at the reopening of the New York Stock Exchange. After one September 11 memorial event, the Senate was abuzz with the story that Schumer was, in the words of one aide, "grandstanding, inserting his face into every picture. Then he tried to get into her limousine, but she has Secret Service and all that. She kept him out. It was a real scene."

Whatever their problems, the senators ultimately hold their differences in check. The potential for friction between Hillary Rodham Clinton and Chuck Schumer is always there, as it is between her and many of her colleagues. But it is unlikely—given the discipline of the Democratic caucus—that much of this friction will spill out into the public domain, as it did with Feingold.

Schumer's dogged courting of the farthest reaches of New York state contrasts another possible danger for Hillary—her intermittent connection with her state.

"We see Chuck all the time," one upstate Democratic county chairman says. "Hillary just seems to appear in big media markets like Rochester and Syracuse." A New York state Republican agrees. "Chuck Schumer's out there every Sunday. He's going to all these markets—B markets—Elmiras, Johnstowns, Oswegos."

Sometimes, even the putative home of Bill and Hillary, in suburban Chappaqua, seems too far from Washington, D.C. "She actually doesn't like being there," a Senate Republican aide says. "She will fly back here [to Washington] rather than spend the night there."

Still, it is difficult to imagine her allowing New York—rural or urban—to slip away. There is plenty of time to get back to Skaneateles to praise the cherry pie.

Who could run against her in 2006? Elliot Spitzer, the super-ambitious New York attorney general and Wall Street *bête noir*, is the only other New York Democrat with the star power and fund-raising potential to rival her in the Democratic primary. He is already holding "Spitzer 2006" events in a transparent bid for George Pataki's governor's seat. Spitzer has every interest in facilitating Hillary's reelection in 2006, and her move up to the White House. Promoting her in Washington is his surest way of keeping her out of his way in Albany.

A far more serious home-state obstacle is Al Sharpton, the Harlem huckster turned presidential candidate. Sharpton's quixotic bid for the presidency, says longtime Republican strategist Roger Stone, is about "running for Jesse"—enhancing his Rolodex and winning respect. "He's becoming the number one black man in America," Stone says. "If he decides to run as an independent for the Senate, she's sunk." Hillary, attuned to political danger like a swallow to a distant storm, appears often with Sharpton, and is obviously out to keep him appeased.

Sharpton's racial demagoguery and persistent cop-baiting, however, carries a price for Hillary. "He's a slug of the highest order," says a former high-ranking New York City official. New York City cops—and voters whose primary concern is law and order—are deeply suspicious of him, and Sharpton's new national profile in Democratic forums is especially problematic for Hillary among rank-and-file police and fire personnel.

Many of Hillary's problems with police and fire personnel are her own fault, however, due to the arms-length relationship she displayed toward law enforcement before September 11, 2001. In terms of statistics, the New York City police department in the days of Rudy Giuliani had an exemplary record of keeping guns in holsters (compared to other large municipal police departments). In terms of public standing, every man and woman in blue felt heat over the shooting of Amadou Diallo, the West African immigrant who was mistakenly shot by New York City police officers when he reached for his wallet. In those heady days, when Bruce Springsteen was crooning "forty-one shots . . . you can get killed just for living/In your American skin," Rudy stood by New York's finest. Hillary headed for the tall grass. "She turned down escorts by uniformed police, for reasons never fully explained," says a former New York law enforcement official. "Why?"

It was likely no surprise to Hillary that there is bad blood between her and police, fire, and other "first responders." Still, the depth of their disdain had to have come as a shock when police and firemen refused to shake her hand at the ruins of the World Trade Center. The antipathy broke out into public display when she appeared at a Paul McCartney benefit concert for New York City on October 20, 2001, when police, fire, and emergency personnel lustily booed her off the stage.

"She was summarily booed by the whole crowd," an eyewitness recalls. "And they were mostly police and fire department folks. Nothing preceded it. It was just her [appearance], like somebody pushed the flint on the lighter. When she left, it stopped as soon as it started." Fireman Mike Moran, who lost a brother in the collapse of the World Trade Center, explained this reaction to radio talk-show host Rush Limbaugh: "I think when times are good and things are going well, people will sit there and listen to the kind of claptrap that comes out of her mouth. When things are going like this, when it's serious times and serious men who actually suffered losses, and she wants to spew her nonsense—she doesn't believe a thing she says. . . . I don't think there's ever been a sincere word that's ever come out of her mouth."[28]

In the general election campaign of 2006, Governor George Pataki—if he chooses to run—might make a formidable opponent. For the moment, however, he is mired in a prodigious state budget meltdown exceeded only by that faced by Gray Davis, the recalled governor of California. The only opponent who should strike fear in the Hillary camp is, of course, Rudy Giuliani. She likely cannot forget the Marist survey showing that Giuliani could demolish her. The question is: Will Giuliani want to risk his global hero status on what would be a bruising campaign? Most incumbent senators are difficult to beat. Hillary—with a huge war chest, planetary name-recognition, and a commanding following among female voters—would be a particularly tough opponent, even for Giuliani. Admirers of the former mayor speculate that he is not actually interested in the Senate, but rather in taking on Spitzer for the governor's mansion in 2006—that is, if he passes up a direct 2008 run for the White House.

Senator Clinton faces another pitfall, the perception that when it comes to serving New York, she is no Daniel Patrick Moynihan.

"She's really dropped the ball for New York," says a prominent woman who worked closely with the late senator on the Environment and Public Works Committee. "If Pat Moynihan were alive today, and still serving in the Senate, New York would have a better infrastructure, would have rebuilt faster after 9/11. Pat had tremendous dedication." Moynihan was adept at logrolling and linking the interests of New York to other states. This observer asserts that he had a political will to push through major projects that Hillary seems to lack.

"You can show up for the hearings and write a 'dear colleague' letter, but the reality of life is you have to be part of the team. I am not sure what team she's on. I understand she wanted to announce his [Moynihan's] death. What I don't understand is: Where is his memorial [in her legislation]? Pat had huge dreams. What has she accomplished?"

Indeed, the centerpiece of Hillary's prescription for the New York economy is a pallid combination of grants and "targeted tax incentives" for job creation and high-tech investments.

On the other hand, unless Giuliani manages to knock her out of the Senate, it is difficult to imagine Hillary losing in a bid for reelection in 2006. She has plenty of time to reconnect with voters, to make high-profile stands for state projects, to once again shower upstate New York with solicitude.

She has every reason to believe that she will only need to present a new persona for her to be accepted. Consider what she has already accomplished. As a result of her most recent reinvention, it is now considered impolite to mention the scandals over those bartered pardons and the furniture that she stole from the White House. There have been no fresh scandals from Hillary's Senate office. The new Hillary does everything right, which is why so many Washington observers are saying that after Bush 43, she is destined to become Clinton 44.

CHAPTER THREE

Livid History

"My father's approach was vintage Hugh Rodham. When I was facing a problem, he would look me straight in the eyes and ask, 'Hillary, how are you going to dig yourself out of this one?' His query always brought to mind a shovel."[1]

—Hillary Rodham Clinton

"THE RAP IS THAT SHE CAN'T FINISH THE BOOK," a well-connected New York literary agent confided. "No one thinks the book will be much of anything. She's pro-war, anti-war, what's she gonna talk about?" The funereal rumors circulating through New York publishing circles were so relentless that they forced Simon & Schuster to deny that the *Living History* manuscript was unfinished, untitled, and heading off the cliff.[2]

"Her publisher paid her an $8 million advance for nothing," said a New York Republican. "Don't they know about her lack of discipline?"

All this talk was forgotten when the book came out in a great orgy of publicity. There was a melodramatic interview with Barbara Walters. Then there were three (!) folksy chats with Katie Couric in Ms.

Couric's trademark perky, perky, cheerleader style. Then commenced the historic coast-to-coast book-signing tour. No authoress in America had ever enjoyed such a Grand Tour.

The first printing alone was an astonishing one million copies. For commuters and, presumably, the illiterate, the book went straight into audio—"As Read by the Author."[3] The industry whose gossips once whispered that she was incapable of finishing a book began whispering that Hillary will likely win a second Grammy (after winning her first for her dramatic rendition of *It Takes a Village*).

Her barnstorming of America with her signing pen had its perils. After one particularly arduous signing session, the *New York Times* reported, "a volunteer administered a vigorous rubbing to revive [her hand]. Senator Clinton soaks it in ice or wears a wrist support to recover."[4] Undaunted, the senator proceeded with "Hillary, the World Tour." Anxious crowds wended around the cobbled streets of London and Berlin to get a glimpse of her. I happened to be in London when she arrived. The book party thrown for her occurred during the height of London's summer season and drew reporters away from even the toniest parties. For much of the week, her interviews filled the quality papers while the tabloids feasted on the squalidities of the Clinton marriage. Within a few weeks, the German translation of *Living History* had sold 120,000 copies, placing the book at number two on *Der Spiegel*'s nonfiction bestseller list.[5]

Why, then, the pre-publication rumors about Hillary's inability to come through? No doubt, there was some truth to the allegation that some executive at Simon & Schuster had a near-death experience— the Clintons are famously tardy. The biggest reason, however, is that the Clinton-watchers were tardy—they were late in adjusting to the fact that a pattern has been broken. Hillary has learned political discipline. Her father's stern approach worked, at least now that she had freed herself from her husband's chaotic milieu. She had kept her Senate race on time and she kept to her publication schedule for her unusual memoir. Senator Clinton is more punctilious than the Hillary who served her husband as first lady. She is infinitely more suave than the first lady whose temper tantrums and rudeness to her staff were staples of White House press coverage and who drew hoots when her earlier book, *It Takes a Village,* arrived in bookstores.

You can appreciate her transformation by noting how she now treats the nuances of being an author. The publishing world had expected her to repeat the famous scandal that followed publication of *It Takes a Village.* Driven by her lifelong instinct to hog the show, Hillary had refused to acknowledge the work of ghostwriter Barbara Feinman.

Sally Quinn, who had used Feinman, a Georgetown journalism teacher, as a researcher said that all Feinman expected "was 'Many thanks to Barbara Feinman, whose tireless efforts were greatly appreciated.' She would have died and gone to heaven." Not only was Feinman not acknowledged in *It Takes a Village,* but she learned that Hillary wanted Simon & Schuster to withhold one-quarter of her $120,000 payment—because Hillary felt that Feinman had not quite delivered. This would have been a cruel blow to a single woman living alone in a one-bedroom apartment, on the verge of going to China to adopt a baby girl. "She was absolutely distraught," Quinn told the *New Yorker.*[6]

Feinman let her distress be known. Rather than propitiate her, however, Hillary went into full war-room mode against the poor woman, summoning journalists to her private White House study to show them reams of legal pads filled with HRC's own handwriting.[7]

Madame Hillary was in charge once again, and the result was not a happy one for her. Feinman got the last word. Reportedly it was she who tipped off Bob Woodward that Hillary was holding "séances" in the White House, communing with the ghost of Eleanor Roosevelt, presumably on the Immensities, possibly universal health care. The nation had another good laugh at Madame Hillary's expense.

With the publication of *Living History*, the evidence suggests that the New Hillary—that is to say, Senator Clinton—has learned from past mistakes. Possibly she has overlearned. In *Living History*, she thanks her three literary helpers. Then her thoughts return to the village. "This book may not have taken a village to write, but it certainly took a superb team," she graciously acknowledges; there follows five pages of acknowledgements.[8] The list includes hundreds of political, advance, and media types, as well as scores of friends. But Hillary still shows no room for compassion or correction. In fact, Madame Hillary reemerges time and again throughout this memoir, in all her chilling anger and self-righteousness. She remembers past slights, petty or large, and reprises deceits, ignoring how thunderously they were exposed during the scandalous 1990s. In *Living History*, Hillary even pauses to take a shot at a minor adversary she should have long ago forgotten, the ghostwriter Feinman. It is 1995, and Madame Hillary marvels at how young Chelsea has matured while First Lady Hillary is immured in the White House family quarters, where she "had to put in long hours writing and enlist help" for *It Takes a Village*.[9] Feinman remains unacknowledged by name.

Living History may read like many other self-serving campaign biographies, but within that literary subgenre, it is well done. "This book and the attendant public relations campaign is a grand inoculation effort," says GOP consultant Philip Kawior. "It is a vehicle with which she brings up her past, debates it on her own terms, earns the right to call it 'old hat,' and removes bad stories as a counterforce for her future ambitions."[10] Kawior's elucidation of how *Living History* deals with Hillary's controversial past is startlingly similar to what seems to be a four-step procedure that the Clintons have developed for refurbishing their records, which, through the years, have so often been in need of refurbishment, namely:

1. Vigorously deny a given charge.
2. Question the motives of an accuser or any accessory to the charge (reporters, prosecutors, victims).
3. Recast the charge in a sweet and melancholy way: "Oh, how sad," or "I don't know if I can go on."
4. Vilify anyone still interested in the charge as an obsessive, a Clinton-hater, a sucker for "old news"—or in Kawior's parlance, "old hat"—all to "remove bad stories as a counterforce for her future ambitions."

The question that will remain unanswered for now is: Will "the grand inoculation effort" work? Many political observers think it will. In *Living History*, Senator Hillary engages in what is at bottom a political, not a literary venture, one that will smooth the way for possible efforts at higher office—and she pocketed $8 million in the bargain.

Her problem is the episodic reappearances of Madame Hillary in an otherwise calm and at times even ladylike narrative. Each time Madame Hillary appears, *Living History* becomes *Livid History*. Given the glamour and excitement Hillary has lived through during her adult life, she could have published a memoir replete with interesting stories that did not hiss and sneer. We see evidence of this in those parts of the book in which Senator Clinton and her new staff of professional political handlers could labor undisturbed by Madame Hillary and ghosts from the past.

In the sections recollecting her youth in Chicago, she lays down a winsome tale of life in innocent suburbia, before the tumult of the late 1960s and 1970s. She tells of riding her bicycle with the other neighborhood children behind the thick fog from city trucks fumigating summer insects. Growing up not far from her in Chicagoland, I remember such youthful adventures poignantly. Only later did we find out that the trucks might have been spraying carcinogens. Then too, *Living History* includes some of Hillary's amusing escapades as first lady. She recounts the time that the Senate's nonagenarian ladies' man, Strom Thurmond, accosted Chelsea, telling the young girl, "You're as pretty as your mama. She's real pretty and you're pretty too. Yes, you are. You're as pretty as your mama." She remembers a red-faced Boris Yeltsin greeting her with a melodious shout, "Heel-lary!" Less amusingly, the bloody tyrant Robert Mugabe giggles like a mad king. And Senator Clinton can turn her party loyalty to amusement too. For instance, she recalls the Republican actor John Wayne in an elevator complaining about the lousy food at the 1968 Republican convention in Miami. At the time Hillary had moved from being a "Goldwater girl" to enjoying an undergraduate flirtation with the Rockefeller wing of the GOP before heading off into the far reaches of the leftist *Kultursmog.*

Senator Clinton also uses her memoir to report such newsworthy moments as her private conversation with Tony and Cherie Blair, which included talk of "French perfidy vis-à-vis Iran and Iraq."[11] Half the book is travelogue—a wise choice, for her many travels present Hillary as a global figure. Her travels relate far more cinematic color in Islamabad and Dublin than could ever be derived from the sterile machinations of her war room against Kenneth Starr. She reports from exotic Katmandu in the Himalayas and scenic Jackson Hole, Wyoming, in a debonair style that suggests at least that her eye for travel would contribute vividly to the pages of the Sunday newspapers' travel sections. On the other hand, too frequently her narrative is jarring. Some of the scenes she revives seem reckless, and an unnecessary disinterment of old scandals.

Consider how, in this memoir, she deals with Dick Morris. Morris, before his reincarnation as a television political analyst, was the political wizard who rescued the Clintons from the policy disasters and faux pas of their first term in the White House, just as he had rescued them from the similar disasters of Bill's first term in the Arkansas governor's mansion. After Republicans captured both houses of Congress, causing a woebegone President Clinton to protest that he remained "relevant," it was Morris who coached Clinton in asserting managerial ambivalence ("triangulation" is the esoteric term they applied to it) and thereby regaining his popularity with contented voters. Then, in July 1996, as Democrats celebrated Morris's achievement at their triumphal national convention, disaster struck. The tabloids— America's newspapers of record during the Clinton years—ambushed Morris with a story about what is politely referred to as a "sex-industry worker" in his room in the Jefferson Hotel. Morris, the prostitute reported, let her listen in on conversations he had with the president. Press reports of Morris's voluptuous multi-tasking while on the telephone with his boss damaged both men. One story, however, particularly galled Hillary for years. It was reported that Morris had bragged to the prostitute that he had written Hillary's successful 1996 convention speech. Hillary uses her memoir to deny it. Look it up, page 377.

The only other first lady in American history who might have been immersed in the kind of setting that requires her to place her word against that of a prostitute is Mrs. Warren G. Harding, and she had the self-restraint to avoid such public discussion. Hillary, being a Coat and Tie Radical, has no self-restraint, of course. A prodigy of the 1960s, she cannot stop talking about herself. Being a 1960s youth, she is sufficiently narcissistic and amoral to remain oblivious as to how her controversies might appear to a wider sector of American life. Aloft in her self-regard, she assumes that the world will share her conviction that she is always blameless, her scandals being always and unquestionably someone else's fault.

Thus, in those angry sections of *Living History*, she revives scandals that might more prudently have been left in the past. To the imperilment of her future political career she brings up such dark chapters in her life as Roger Clinton's drug dealings, the FBI files on Republicans that appeared in the White House on a former saloon bouncer's desk, her theory that Vince Foster's death was caused by the *Wall Street Journal*, the fair sex's obsession with her virginal husband, Bill's dialogue with Monica, her own luck with cattle futures, and the intricacies of Travelgate. In doing so, she revives issues that could cloud Senator Clinton's future, for surely they will remind readers of her instinctive aversion to the truth and of her easy abuses of power. In light of the damning evidence against her in independent counsel Robert Ray's final report, she is particularly reckless about Travelgate and Whitewater, apparently trusting in the restorative power of the Clintons' Four-Step Formula for refurbishing the record. The problem is that after a decade of scandals and exposés, there is now so much evidence revealing her culpability that only a Clinton true believer will be satisfied by her protestations to innocence.

Most of the true believers are from the left of the political spectrum. They have made belief in the Clintons' innocence a Noble Cause, much as they once made belief in Alger Hiss's innocence a Noble Cause. The guilt of Hiss was irrefragably established when Soviet archives were opened. Friends of Senator Clinton have reason to fear that her guilt is irrefragably established when her memoir is opened. Her friends might also fear that *Livid History* displays one of Hillary's intellectual quirks that had best be kept offstage: her conspiratorial mindset, her insistence that in politics she has been confronted not with policy disagreements but with conspiracies, vast, right-wing conspiracies.

When the memoir came out, Barbara Walters gave Hillary an opportunity, during an ABC interview, to step back from her conspiratorial broodings by asking whether the first lady still believed the Lewinsky scandal was the product of a "vast right-wing conspiracy." "I would say that there is a very well-financed right-wing network of people. It's not really conspiracy because it's pretty much out in the light of day, that was after his presidency from the very beginning, really stopped at nothing, even to the point of perverting the Constitution, in order to undermine what he was trying to do for the country," she replied.[12] This, to an informed observer, brings to mind the late liberal historian Richard Hofstadter's brilliant 1964 essay, "The Paranoid Style in American Politics." Yet Hofstadter identified "the paranoid style" with conservatism. Now Hillary and a growing number of her allies are evincing these paranoid symptoms on the left. For years, political observers might well have wondered if a left-wing equivalent of the John Birch Society were possible. Hillary, with her belief in conspiracies, has demonstrated that it is. The only difference is that no Bircher will ever bid fair to dominate the Republican Party.

Hillary dominates the Democratic Party today, so much so that even its party chairman squawks about the conspiracies against them.

In *Livid History*, Madame Hillary appears to be selective about the skeletons she releases from the Clinton closet. She repeats the Clintons' soap-opera version of Roger Clinton's drug conviction and her version of Filegate, possibly thinking that in the former instance the soap-opera story remains plausible and beguiling, and that in the latter instance she can fix the record with a Four-Step refurbishment. In both cases she is oblivious to 1990s revelations. For Madame Hillary to bring these matters up again is imprudent in the extreme.

The story of Roger Clinton's 1984 arrest and subsequent conviction on drug charges has been used by the Clintons for years, supposedly to demonstrate Bill's probity. According to their script, Bill as governor stood aside, allowing drug investigators to conduct the sting that nabbed Roger. After Roger's conviction, a tearful governor appeared on the courthouse steps, saying, "I feel more deeply committed than ever before to do everything I can to fight drugs in our state." Says Hillary now in her memoir, "Bill and I berated ourselves for not seeing signs of Roger's abuse and taking some kind of action to help him."[13] Unfortunately for the Clintons, much more came out during the 1990s about recreational drug use in Little Rock during Bill's tenure in the governor's mansion. Her brief two paragraphs ignoring her husband's deeper involvement in the scandal deals her reputation for honesty another blow. Half a dozen or more Arkansans have testified to doing drugs with both Clinton brothers or to witnessing them doing drugs. In fact, it now has widely been reported that during Roger's investigation he was videotaped saying, "I've got to get some for my brother, he's got a nose like a Hoover vacuum cleaner." The officer who conducted the sting claims Governor Clinton shut it down prematurely to protect himself from being implicated in drugs.[14] If this videotape is inaccurate, Hillary might at least say so. As a consequence of the 1984 sting, not only Roger but also a friend and major financial supporter of the Clintons, Dan Lasater, went to jail briefly before being pardoned by the governor. Arkansas state troopers and others have testified that Lasater supplied cocaine to Bill at raucous Arkansas parties. There is no Lasater in *Livid History*. For the good of Senator Clinton's future, there should have been no mention of Roger's drug use or of the legend the Clintons confected about Bill. It is one more example of Hillary's reckless mendacity.

Another skeleton Madame Hillary imprudently drags from the closet is Filegate. In 1996, when the aforementioned former barroom bouncer and Democratic dirty tricks practitioner Craig Livingstone was caught in the White House with over nine hundred FBI security files on past Republican White House aides, Hillary denied any knowledge of the fact. In *Livid History* she gratuitously disinters the scandal, disparaging it as a "pseudoscandal." Yet by now witnesses have testified under oath that the files were meant for partisan political intelligence and that Livingstone's employment at the White House's Office of Personnel Security came about after the First Lady's recommendation.[15] When an FBI agent critical of placing a man with Livingstone's unsavory background in such a serious security role voiced his skepticism to associate White House counsel William Kennedy, this former law partner of Hillary told the agent, "It's a done deal. Hillary wants him."[16] Despite testimony from others and affidavits such as this, Madame Hillary keeps grinding the ax in *Livid History*. Yet the evidence against her is too stark to be wished away.

On some skeletons, however, Hillary remains reticent. In her treatment of Vince Foster, for instance, she never addresses charges that have now been deposed on the public record. Foster was her longtime partner at Arkansas's now defunct Rose Law Firm. He accompanied her to Washington as deputy White House counsel. After his body was found in Fort Marcy Park in July 1993, there were reports he committed suicide because he feared the coming revelations about the Clintons' business practices and their tax evasions or because relations with Hillary had become painful. Arkansas state troopers detailed to the governor's mansion had spoken in 1993 of Hillary's maintaining an on-again, off-again love affair with him. In Washington, she froze him out, believing that he was not up to defending the Clintons from prying eyes. That alleged affair is not refuted, though she continues to blame his death on an editorial in the *Wall Street Journal.* This lapse into paranoia had best been repressed.

Most of the skeletons she does address reveal Madame Hillary's unpleasantness as she grinds axes, settles scores, and attempts to refurbish a record that, given the intervening years of revelations, is beyond refurbishment and best ignored. In each instance she perpetrates a deceit that is obvious. Or tells an unnecessary lie. Or reminds us of scandals that were well behind her until the publication of *Livid History.* Deceits, lies, and bullying are recurrent themes in her life, first noted for the public record by Jerome Zeifman, the Democratic counsel to the House Judiciary Impeachment Inquiry in 1974, when he wrote in his personal evaluation of her that he "could not recommend her for any future position of public or private trust. A number of the procedures she recommended were ethically flawed. And I also concluded that she had violated House and committee rules by disclosing confidential information to unauthorized persons."[17]

In his 1995 book on the impeachment of President Richard Nixon, Zeifman twice emphasizes Hillary's dishonesty, once adjudging that she was "unworthy of either public or private trust,"[18] and later declaring that she had a propensity for "misleading, if not deceiving, Congress."[19] Some of her lies have been amusing, for instance, the delightful little lie she tried out on a New Zealand audience while she was first lady. It was totally gratuitous. She confided to the assembled Auklanders that she had been named after Sir Edmund Hillary, their beloved conqueror of Mount Everest. This is truly remarkable. Hillary was born in 1947, six years before Edmund Hillary climbed Mount Everest. At the time, the great adventurer was still an obscure beekeeper.

Then, of course, there are the large lies she has told in her life, some of which are equally gratuitous. Probably the most famous large and gratuitous lie told by Madame Hillary in *Livid History* is the one that gained attention even before the book was published. This is her claim that she believed her husband's repeated protests of innocence during the seven months between intern Monica Lewinsky's national debut and the forty-second president's wretched admission in August that he had used her as his comfort woman. Here again, no lie is necessary and to attempt a whopper is arrantly reckless. Of course, Hillary had to address her husband's impeachment and his affair with Lewinsky in her memoir. But she could have employed tact rather than egregious lies. Surely no reader would fault Hillary had she written something to the effect that when the story of Lewinsky's affair first came out her heart was broken. Emotions overcame her intellect. As a loving wife, she accepted the rogue's claim that he had only been ministering to a young girl's "emotional needs." A little lie such as that would be sufficient, and she could pass on to the happier moments of *Living History*. Instead, Madame Hillary applies her Four-Step Formula to the public record, offering up a sweet and melancholy tale and heaving in a colossal lie that not even a Clinton true believer would swallow.

She actually writes that when her lawyer, Bob Barnett, warned her on August 14, 1998, that the president might be on the verge of admitting that he had lied about Monica, she said, "Look, Bob. My husband may have his faults, but he has never lied to me." Then comes the soap opera. She writes that Bill awoke her the next morning and admitted his "inappropriate intimacy" with Lewinsky (Inappropriate? It included being fellated by Lewinsky during his telephone conversation with a congressman. The topic was troop deployments in Bosnia.) Curtain up: "I could hardly breathe. Gulping for air, I started crying and yelling at him, 'What do you mean? What are you saying? Why did you lie to me?'"[20]

Lewinsky's relationship as reported months before was precisely the kind of relationship Clinton had been having for years in Arkansas and was now apparently having in Washington, right down to the trademark Clinton biblical exegesis about oral sex not being adultery. Just four years before Monica's revelations, Arkansas state troopers in the pages of the *American Spectator* described assignations between Clinton and women, some of them being government employees, that involved precisely the same sex acts that Monica revealed. Surely when the story came out that a White House intern was servicing her husband Hillary knew it was true, but sticking to her time-tested tactic, she tops off her lies by impugning those who exposed the scandal. "For me," she writes, "the Lewinsky imbroglio seemed like just another vicious scandal manufactured by political opponents."[21]

Her opponents had manufactured nothing. *Living History* had not been out a week before critics were citing published accounts of her behavior back in the summer of 1998 that refuted Hillary's claims.

They cited the *Washington Post*'s Peter Baker, who in his 2000 book, *The Breach*, established that Clinton lawyer David Kendall tipped Hillary off at least a day before Barnett spoke to her. As for the soap-opera "gulping," "crying," and "yelling," the Clintons' most loyal true believer, Sidney Blumenthal, reported in his 2003 memoir, *The Clinton Wars,* that Hillary was at peace with her ithyphallic husband just forty-eight hours after his nationally televised confession of August 15. Sidney writes of receiving a telephone call from the Clintons on August 17 seeking his reaction to Bill's televised admission: "Hillary asked me what I thought. . . . The President was pleased with it. Hillary also approved. That was the most important thing of all." The Clintons handed the telephone over to James Carville and their pollster, Mark Penn, and Sidney recalls, "I could hear the President and Hillary bantering in the background. . . . [T]hey were still working as a team."[22]

Hillary's knowledge of her husband's cheating has been the oldest running theme of their relationship. *Living History* makes no mention of many key people in her life who have confirmed this truth in books, in interviews, and at times under threat of prosecution. Her memoir continues her years of dissembling and covering up. As she considers her future electoral prospects, Hillary perhaps has justification for continuing to play down Bill's endless adulterous couplings, though the issue cuts both ways. If she took the opposite stance, she could always present herself to feminists as a victim of the male penile imperative.

The problem here is that she has not been a victim but rather a classic enabler. Speaking of Hillary's role during her husband's carousals in the 1980s, former Arkansas state auditor Julia Hughes Jones says, "Every time he was out and Hillary knew where he went, she would call behind him to see what she needed to do to take care of it."[23] Her involvement as an accessory to her husband's behavior continued right onto the national stage. In his memoir, *All Too Human,* George Stephanopoulos depicts Hillary leading the war room's smear campaign against Gennifer Flowers, whose audiotape of Bill coaching his former lover to lie to the press put such a scare into the Clintons' first presidential campaign. Bill's coaching Gennifer, caught on that tape, would be echoed five years later in Monica Lewinsky's testimony. Lewinsky described how President Clinton coached her to lie and obstruct justice during his 2 a.m. call from the White House, four weeks before their affair became a national delectation. Themes of obstruction and deceit have repeated themselves in the Clintons' lives for thirty years.

Other accounts of life with the Clintons have established the bizarre reality of their marriage. Two early associates of the Clintons who have testified to their faithless marriage are Paul and Mary Lee Fray, the team that ran Bill's failed 1974 bid for Congress. When Hillary first arrived in Arkansas, Bill was, as they say in those parts, "carrying on" with a student volunteer from Fayetteville. In the midst of his campaigning, Clinton somehow managed to keep track of his two girlfriends, asking Mary Lee to sneak the local girl out the back door of their campaign headquarters whenever Hillary arrived at the front door.[24]

In *Living History,* Hillary retells the old Clinton legend that while she was laboring in Washington on Nixon's impeachment, her Republican father rustled up her brothers and headed off to the Confederacy to campaign for her fiancé in the Arkansas backcountry. This was a plausible and serviceable legend during the 1970s and 1980s. Unfortunately, during the 1990s, the Clintons' legends were subjected to closer scrutiny. David Maraniss portrays the Rodhams' mission more accurately in *First in His Class,* his 1996 biography of Bill. He says they were there to keep an eye on Bill and act as a barrier between him and the girls. According to Maraniss, "[A]side from the Fayetteville woman, the staff also knew that Clinton had girlfriends in several towns around the district and in Little Rock." He quotes Paul Fray to the effect that, "Hillary had put the hammer on her daddy to go down there and make sure everything was hunky-dory. It was her little spying mission."[25] Fray also recounts Hillary's crying jags and the arguments between the young couple over Bill's roaming interests.[26]

In late 1993, the *Los Angeles Times* and the *American Spectator* published the testimony of some of the much-maligned Arkansas state troopers attesting to Clinton's inveterate womanizing. Books continue to come out listing Bill's cavalcade of adultery. If readers are surprised by the revelations to date, wait a few more years. As with the Kennedys, the books chronicling the Clintons' errancies are going to fill whole library shelves. Hillary's energetic dissembling about Bill's licentiousness will not serve her well in the years ahead. Even now, it is known that in 1988, Senator Gary Hart's sex scandal in part deterred Bill from joining the presidential race. Clinton's philandering was of such a concern to his gubernatorial chief of staff, Betsey Wright, that she would often call his hotel room late at night just to see if he would answer.[27] According to Maraniss, a list of Bill's paramours drawn up by Wright also helped persuade the Arkansas governor to pass on running in 1988. Maraniss confirms that Wright "said that he was having a serious affair with another woman, and was not even being discreet about it. Everyone knew, she said. She knew, the troopers knew, Hillary knew. There were great screaming matches at the mansion. Once a counselor was called out to mediate. Clinton was broaching the subject of divorce in conversations with some of his colleagues, governors from other states who had survived the collapse of their marriages. But he told his friends in Arkansas that he wanted to save his marriage. And Hillary wanted to save it, too. She told Wright that she was unwilling to abandon the partnership. She had invested too much in Bill Clinton and was determined to see it through."[28]

There is a comic majesty to Hillary's ongoing lies about her husband's well-established goatishness. In comparative terms, only the Clinton true believers surpass her. Writes Madame Hillary after the Lewinsky affair first broke into the news, "Bill told me that Monica Lewinsky was an intern he had befriended." She "had asked him for some job-hunting help." It gets better: "This was completely in character for Bill. He said that she had misinterpreted his attention, which was something I had seen happen dozens of times before. It was such a familiar scenario that I had little trouble believing the accusations were groundless. By then, I also had endured more than six years of baseless claims. . . ."[29] These things happen in every presidency. President William McKinley had a particularly difficult time fending off starry-eyed interns after his kind-hearted counseling sessions. Richer still is the explanation of how Bill suffered at the hands of those infamous Arkansas state troopers. In a book that is considered by the Clinton faithful to be the official history of the Clinton scandals, Joe Conason, one of Hillary's truest believers, explains that back in Arkansas the governor's chief of staff had her hands full: "What had always bothered Betsey Wright most about the troopers was their bad influence on Clinton himself. She disliked their boozing and womanizing most of all. Keeping sexually adventurous women away from Bill Clinton had been a staff preoccupation. . . ." The troopers, " 'exploited his sexual attractiveness to women,' Wright said. . . ."[30] Then the impressionable governor became president and an entire nation of "adventurous women" headed to Washington.

By now even Clinton true believers are curious about the dynamic of the fractious Clinton marriage. Millions of Americans wonder how Bill and Hillary have remained free of the divorce lawyers. The marriage is a very cosmopolitan arrangement, more typical of European jet-set society than of America. It is a playboy marriage, the kind Profirio Rubirosa glided into with Doris Duke. True, at a certain practical level it is the marriage of convenience I described in *Boy Clinton,* allowing both Clintons to advance their political ambitions as they avail themselves of each other's uncommon political skills. Yet there is an emotional side too, deeply fulfilling to both parties' idiosyncratic needs. Bill's waywardness gives Hillary ample opportunities to exercise Madame Hillary's indignant bossiness. And Madame Hillary's tireless watchfulness allows Bill exciting opportunities to sneak out on mother. Bill is, after all, a mama's boy, and Hillary is the vigilant overseer of her errant charge. An anecdote reported to the *American Spectator* by an Arkansas state trooper guarding the Clintons in the 1980s suggests the drama. Hillary is a heavy sleeper, and Bill was wont to undertake nocturnal trysts. One night, she awoke at a late hour to find the governor AWOL. Knowing immediately what was up, she called down to the trooper in the guardhouse. Told that the governor had gone out for a drive, she exclaimed, "The sorry son of a bitch!" That was the trooper's cue to get Bill home, which he did by calling his boss on his cell phone. Reaching him at a woman's home, he related the bad news: Hillary would be waiting for him. "Oh god, god, what did you tell her?" the little rascal inquired. When he got home, she ambushed him in the kitchen. Later, the trooper found the kitchen "a wreck, with a cabinet door kicked off its hinges."[31] All things considered, this has been a happy marriage. That it might end abruptly as the parties mature is always possible. A quick divorce could help Hillary with the feminist vote and with those independents who insist right and wrong matter.

The late Michael Kelly, who for perceiving the Clintons so insightfully has gained revilement from them even in his grave, wrote after the Monica debacle, "Mrs. Clinton is to some degree a victim, and she is to be pitied for this. But is Mrs. Clinton entirely a victim, or is she also, with her husband, a victimizer of the rest of us?"[32]

Even in the fury of his prose, Kelly was too much the gentleman to say the obvious. Hillary is nobody's victim.

The Unindicted Co-President

There are other episodes in Hillary's memoir that might have benefited from the crisp, clean, businesslike treatment of Senator Clinton rather than the self-absorbed Four-Step refurbishment practiced by Madame Hillary. The old deceits do not wear well when placed beside, say, the final report of independent counsel Robert Ray. Moreover, Madame Hillary's continued slanders of Ray's predecessor, Kenneth Starr, are ungracious. Truth be known, she and her husband owe him a lot. Starr and his predecessor, Robert Fiske, raised the Clintons from the rank of being two querulous mediocrities camped atop a national monument, akin to the Hardings, to the highest rank attainable in modern America, celebrity status. Were it not for the government investigations, prosecutions, and indictments, the Clintons might merely be remembered as the White House tenants who neglected the Rev. Osama bin Laden and as the Democrats who made Republican reforms work for them. But from their notoriety as subpoena dodgers and obstructers of justice came the celebrity status that is more crucial to their lush publishing advances than anything ever perpetrated by them in politics. Without their celebrity and the rich cast of characters Starr revealed in his modern Rabelaisian classic, the *Starr Report*, the Clintons would be but shabby heirs to Richard Nixon, mere wretches with law licenses suspended, friends in jail, impeachment in the résumé. Nor would they be honored with the laurels for foreign policy mastery that the Watergate president achieved. Of the Whitewater couple it can be said that the investigations of them and the convictions of their friends allowed notoriety to crystallize into celebrity, eclipsing their ignominy and transforming them into the Democrats' last glimpse of Roosevelt. Thanks to Ken Starr's exertions, Bill can even boast of the kind of martyrdom that made Alger Hiss a liberal icon. Starr gets no thanks, not even a reference in *Living History*'s acknowledgments.

Instead, Hillary says of his work that "Whitewater came to represent a limitless investigation of our lives that cost the taxpayers over $70 million for the Independent Counsel investigation alone and never turned up any wrong doing on our part. Bill and I voluntarily cooperated with investigators. Every time they leaked...."[33] By the time she wrote that, or her "team" wrote that, Judge Norma Holloway Johnson had received a special master's report on the Clintons' and their lawyer, David Kendall's, allegation that the independent counsel leaked throughout the investigations. Although the report remains under seal, Judge Johnson's court dismissed every one of the Clintons' allegations. As to Hillary's smug assertion that she "voluntarily" cooperated with investigators, again, the record refutes her. Anyone vaguely familiar with her years spent frustrating the independent counsel's legally authorized investigations is aware of the Clintons' assertions of lawyer-client privilege, which the courts threw out; their claims of

Secret Service privilege, which, again, got the courts' heave-ho; the subpoenaed Whitewater billing documents that disappeared into the White House for two years before mysteriously turning up in Hillary's quarters; and, finally, the payment of almost one million dollars that associate attorney general Web Hubbell received after his resignation—money investigators viewed as hush money.

Madame Hillary suggests a vast exoneration of herself in the most sanctimonious leaves of *Livid History* (the independent counsel "never turned up any wrong doing on our part"), but the rebutting evidence from independent counsel Ray's final 2000 report is colossal; this is Madame Hillary lying in high gear. The report sourly concluded, "This office determined that the evidence was insufficient to prove to a jury beyond a reasonable doubt that either President or Mrs. Clinton knowingly participated in any criminal conduct." However, it then asserted that the Clintons were unresponsive or dilatory "involving both the production of relevant evidence and the filing of legal claims that were ultimately rejected by the courts." Of Hillary's husband, Ray said that another reason he decided against prosecution was because "non-criminal" penalties were sufficient. One such penalty turned out to be Bill's disbarment.[34] Additionally, Clinton paid a $25,000 fine for dismissal of a disbarment suit by the Southeastern Legal Foundation and $850,000 to settle the Paula Corbin Jones sexual harassment suit. The judge in that suit found Hillary's husband in contempt of court for "intentionally false testimony," that "undermined the judicial system," and she awarded more than $90,000 in expenses to Mrs. Jones. Yet Hillary tells her readers "no wrong doing on our part" was found? This, Hillary calls exoneration?[35]

More evidence gainsaying Hillary's claims to innocence arrived in the summer of 2003, when three former prosecutors took the extraordinary step of writing a letter to the *Washington Post* to set the record straight from their perspective. The letter will not go unnoticed in Hillary's future political campaigns. They wrote, "As a result of these investigations, a sitting president admitted to providing false and misleading testimony that prejudiced the administration of justice and was cited for contempt of court.

- "He and his wife were found to have given false testimony in more than one aspect of criminal investigations requested by the president's own attorney general.
- "His former business partner was convicted of fraudulently operating a savings and loan at a cost to taxpayers of $73 million.
- "His wife's former law partner, then the associate attorney general of the United States and 11 others, including the sitting governor of Arkansas, were convicted of, and several were imprisoned for, various federal crimes. . . . "[36]

The independent counsel law contains a provision allowing for the reimbursement of an unindicted defendant's legal expenses, and in the aftermath of Whitewater the Clintons qualified for such a reimbursement, for neither was ever indicted. The three-judge panel that decided on their reimbursements did not seem to share Hillary's assurance in *Living History* that investigators "never turned up any wrong doing on our part." Whereas past panels had granted President George H. W. Bush $272,000, or 59 percent of the money he had sought in the aftermath of Iran-Contra, and President Ronald Reagan $562,000, or 72 percent of the amount he had requested, the Clintons' received 2 percent. The three-judge panel averred this unhappy conclusion: "We harbor no doubt that in the absence of the independent counsel statute the allegations surrounding the Clintons, Madison Guaranty and Whitewater would have been similarly investigated and prosecuted by the Department of Justice."[37]

There are other horrors that Hillary should have left in the closet rather than mention in her memoir. In the simpering tones of Madame Hillary, she writes, "I was willing to risk $1,000 and let Jim [Jim Blair, lawyer for Don Tyson of Tyson Foods, the Arkansas chicken producer whose waste management was treated so benignly during the Clinton governorship] guide my trades through the colorfully named broker Robert 'Red' Bone. Red was a former poker player, which made perfect sense, given his calling."[38] There were ups and downs, but then "I got pregnant with Chelsea in 1979," and "lost my nerve for gambling." "I walked away from the table $100,000 ahead." That was a ten thousand percent return for Hillary.[39]

The late Barbara Olson examined Madame Hillary's good fortune. She reported that if Hillary had put her $1,000 into Microsoft stock in 1986, she would have made $35,839. "The premier technology investment of our times, therefore, pales in comparison to what she had made on the world's oldest commodity; livestock." The likelihood of such a return on such an investment was close to lottery odds, twenty-four chances in a million.[40]

Olson concluded: "Unless you believe in good fairies, luck had nothing to do with it. It is pretty obvious that Hillary had something better than luck. She had well-placed friends who wanted her to have $100,000."[41] During this period, Tyson's companies received $8 million in tax concessions and the right, under a seemingly tough environmental governor, to sluice a river of chicken feces through a small town in Arkansas while Hillary and Mr. Bone were playing poker.[42]

Finally, *Living History* would have been less risky had Madame Hillary handled Travelgate more demurely. The scandal of Travelgate involved the Clintons' firing of non-political employees at the White House travel office. Hillary subsequently lied under oath when she testified that she had nothing to do with these firings. Investigators turned up documents and testimony refuting her. The most damning document was a memo written up by White House aide David Watkins. He wrote it as a letter to White House chief of staff Mack McLarty. It reads: "Foster told me that it was important that I speak directly with the First Lady.... I called her that evening and she conveyed to me in clear terms her desire for swift and clear action to resolve the situation. She mentioned that Thomason had explained how the Travel Office could be run after removing the current staff... in light of that she thought immediate action was in order...."

And more: "At that meeting you explained that this was on the First Lady's radar screen. The message you conveyed to me was clear: immediate actions must be taken.... We both knew that there would be hell to pay... if we failed to take swift and decisive action in conformity with the First Lady's wishes."

Despite such evidence weighing against her, Madame Hillary writes in *Living History* that "seven separate investigations" failed to turn up "any illegality, wrongdoing or conflicts of interest...."[43] Ray's final report is not so sanguine. "Mrs. Clinton's input into the process was a significant," the report concludes, "—if not the significant—factor influencing the pace of events in the travel office firings and the ultimate decision to fire the employees." It finds her sworn denials "factually inaccurate." Ray decided against prosecution as the evidence "is insufficient to show that Mrs. Clinton knowingly intended to influence the travel office decision." Again, Madame Hillary would have been better advised not to bring all this up again. Her record for mendacity is only emphasized by the facts.[44]

There is one subject that Hillary did keep out of her memoir, though it might be brought up in future elections. It is a matter in which her role as enabler to Bill reveals how cold she truly is. It is the Juanita Broaddrick story, and *Living History* brought it again into the public eye. Hillary's prevarications in *Livid History* caused Broaddrick to break her silence for the first time since her 1999 interview with Lisa Myers. In that interview, she first told her detailed, credible, and at least partly verifiable story about being raped by Bill Clinton—then the Arkansas attorney general and the state's highest law enforcement officer.

Broaddrick, interviewed on FOX News Channel's *Hannity & Colmes* television program, described an encounter with Hillary Clinton.

BROADDRICK: They [the Clintons] came in, but just before they did, the driver, who was a—who had gone to the airport and picked them up came over to me and said that—he was a local pharmacist in this area and I think he's relocated now in Tefavor, but he told me, he said the whole topic of conversation from the airport was you and are you going to be there? And . . .

HANNITY: This is a friend of yours, the driver?

BROADDRICK: Yes.

HANNITY: And he told you that?

BROADDRICK: He came over to me and said that, and I really didn't know what to think about that. The minute they came in the door, I'm standing over in the living room area and I see them come through the kitchen area, and I see her going up to someone and they're pointing at me. And I see him go the opposite direction. I assumed when they came in if I was still there that he might come up and say something, but she made her way just as quick as she could to me.

HANNITY: And what happened?

BROADDRICK: Well, I almost got nauseous when she came over to me. And she came over to me, took ahold of my hand and said, "I've heard so much about you. And I've been dying to meet you" or been wanting to meet you, I can't—it's just paraphrasing right now. And she said, "I just want you to know how much Bill and I appreciate what you do for him." And I said, "Well, thank you." And I started to turn and walk away. This woman—this little soft spoken—pardon me for the phrase—dowdy woman, that seemed very unassertive, took ahold of my hand and squeezed it. And said, "Do you understand everything that you do?" I could have passed out at that moment. And I got my hand from hers and I left.

HANNITY: How hard was she—she was really squeezing?

BROADDRICK: Yes. She was just holding onto my hand. She didn't—because I had started to turn away from her. And she held onto my hand and she said, "Do you understand everything that you do?" I mean, cold chills went up my spine. That's the first time I became afraid of that woman.[45]

Hillary Rodham Clinton is a feminist who averts her eye from the foulest treatment of women, a once-youthful and tireless investigator of Watergate whose war room surpasses the maddest schemes of the White House Plumbers, the scourge of the establishment who herself works the system for petty gain, long after she has obtained great wealth.

But then, Hillary, in her own mind, can do no wrong. And if she believes this, it is because of experience. Hillary, like a cat, always lands on her feet.

The Resilient Radical

A personal inspection of the public's reaction to *Livid History* proves the point. On a cool evening in early summer 2003, a line made up of more than one thousand adults snaked around a small shopping mall in the Republican-leaning suburb of McLean, Virginia. They were mostly young professional types: a sprinkling of lawyers, accountants, realtors, CIA employees just off duty from the nearby headquarters, and a lot of retirees. Aside from the odd protester (some of them were very odd—especially the fellow carrying a sign reading "If Osama had been a woman, Clinton would have found his ass by now")—these suburbanites were waiting hours in line to meet Hillary Rodham Clinton and to buy her new memoir.

It is hard to remember now, but two years before this, Hillary would have been about as attractive to many of these same people as a mosquito bearing the West Nile virus.

First, there had been the recriminations over her too-clever-by-half manipulation of Senate rules so that she could collect an $8 million advance for this memoir. Then there had been the Clintons' notorious exit from 1600 Pennsylvania. In the last hours of his presidency, Clinton had shocked America by insolently commuting thirty-six prison sentences and handing out 140 pardons to a collection of crooks, some of whom had been conspicuous in the Arkansas underworld. Brother Roger Clinton, himself a convicted drug dealer, was caught peddling some of the pardons. Even high-level felon Susan McDougal got a pardon, a prodigiously bold affront, given Clinton's solemn vow at the height of the Whitewater controversy never to pardon her for her defiance of independent counsel Kenneth Starr. Others on the list shocked the nation, for instance, the fugitive billionaire Marc Rich. His ex-wife, Denise, had become a major Democratic donor just prior to his pardon, giving one million dollars to the Democratic Party and an "enormous sum" (according to her lawyer's boast) to the Clinton Library. Taint from the scandal sullied Hillary directly when it transpired that an aide from her Senate campaign had arranged pardons for members of a New York Hasidic community who had swindled the government out of millions of dollars. Months before, their entire community had voted for Hillary en masse: 1,359 for Hillary, ten against. Equally unseemly, Hugh Rodham, her brother, had arranged pardons for a notorious drug dealer and a swindler after the two men gave him $400,000 in payoffs.

Concomitant with the last-minute pardons came the appalling news that the Clintons had $30,000 worth of White House furniture and flatware packed into the moving vans headed for their new home in Chappaqua, New York. Even longtime supporters in the media such as the *New York Times* and the *Washington Post* railed against Hillary now, and one of her friendliest newspapers asked her to hand back her senatorship. Said the *New York Observer,* "Hillary Rodham Clinton is unfit for elective office. Had she any shame, she would resign. . . ." Of her husband, the *Observer* wrote, "the image that presents itself is terrifyingly close to the caricature his enemies drew of him."[46]

Yet by the summer of 2003, *Livid History* was received ecstatically. As with the Clintons' earlier scandals, their scandals of late 2000 and early 2001 would paralyze an ordinary politician and probably finish him off. Think of what one $4.5 million book deal did to Newt Gingrich's career—and Newt's deal amounted to about half of Hillary's take. In 2003, their exit scandals, once condemned, are remembered only by the conscientious, and the conscientious run the risk of being dismissed as "Clinton-haters." The media that not long before had inveighed mightily against the Clintons were again suffering Clinton-induced amnesia. The national orgy of publicity that launched Hillary's memoir would have been impossible without the amnesiacs in the press. Ever since the Clintons became national figures, the press has alternated from righteous indignation over their lapses to oafish forgetfulness.

The resiliency of the Clintons is without precedent in American history or, for that matter, any history that I am aware of. The disrepute Hillary suffered in 2001 had been suffered before, for instance, after the mishandling of nine hundred confidential background investigations of Republicans from the previous two administrations, after the ransacking of Vince Foster's office after his suicide, after her subpoenaed records disappeared from the White House (and after they reappeared in her White House residence), or after the firing of White House Travel Office employees, or after revelations about Whitewater or her cattle future trades. The Clintons' supporters and the journalists always forgive and forget, mainly forget.

If Hillary has been Bill's enabler, the leftist *Kultursmog* puffed by the liberal media and its auxiliaries enables them both, protective of the Clintons as its own, poisonous to the free exchange of ideas, oppressive to anything new and untainted by its *smog*. The Clintons have understood the *Kultursmog* as a hygienist understands the mold in a tenement's dank cellar. The *Kultursmog* has assisted in their refurbishment of past scandals and exposed lies.

Ultimately, this is the meaning of the reception of *Livid History,* and is its standing warning to conservatives: Nothing's going to change.

CHAPTER FOUR

An Ideological Life

"Wonderfully well researched and organized.
As you appear headed for law school, we will no doubt in
time hear more of your organizing efforts!"

—Hillary's thesis adviser, 1969

IT SHOULD HAVE BEEN THE KIND OF NEWS that stops a nation for a moment of quiet reflection. It was not—but only because the death of retired senator Daniel Patrick Moynihan was completely overshadowed by the early, anxious days of the Iraq War.

He had been hospitalized in January 2003, for an intestinal malady. Then he was in for a back injury. Then again, he was hospitalized for emergency surgery after suffering a ruptured appendix, and a subsequent infection in March. It all proved too much for the retired, four-term senator. He slipped away on March 26, 2003.

The Senate, somewhat like the executive branch, has an ancient code by which it honors its own. There are, of course, no funereal parades, no muffled drums, no horse-drawn caissons. There is only the simple, touching rite of the death announcement—really, a eulogy—brought to the floor of the Senate by the senior senator from the deceased former member's home state. Tradition still rules the Senate. In the early twenty-first century, the men and women who sit in chairs once occupied by Clay, Webster, and Calhoun may be camera-ready, but they still hold fast to the customs of their predecessors.

In Moynihan's case, the death should have been announced by the senior senator from New York, Chuck Schumer. Moreover, in courtesy and common decency, that announcement should have been held back until the late senator's family first had a chance to issue a statement to the press.

The Moynihan family dutifully called both New York Senate offices, informing them of the death, and of their plans to make an announcement at a time convenient to the family. Hillary Rodham Clinton—the junior senator from New York—darted out of a meeting upon hearing of her predecessor's death. "Clinton could barely contain herself with the news," a Senate Democratic staffer said. "She practically ran out the door to make the announcement."[1]

Several hours before the Moynihan family could break the news and Schumer could make the formal announcement to his colleagues, Hillary strode to the Senate floor to make a pretty little speech praising her predecessor. "Schumer was out of his mind," a Senate staffer said. "The family was very upset."[2] "That wasn't hers to announce," a family representative told at least one journalist. "It was classless."[3]

It was more than classless. It was yet another bold rewriting of history, and something even bolder—another operation in the refurbishment of the Clinton record from radical of yesteryear to moderate senator and, perhaps, centrist candidate for the presidency. You would never have known from her florid eulogy that Hillary had once openly despised Moynihan. His party loyalty won her his endorsement, but she never won his respect.

At Wellesley, Hillary's undergraduate thesis was an admiring paper on radical organizer Saul Alinsky, accepting his claims that poverty was the result of a malevolent power structure that needed to be overthrown. Old-fashioned liberals like Daniel Patrick Moynihan were part of the problem. Moynihan was a spokesman for an oppressive class system.

"Moynihan writes in a spirited style," the young Hillary notes, "but even his behind-the-scenes stance does not make his argument less confusing."

She writes that Moynihan "seems to miss the point" on anti-poverty programs, and fails to define his key terms—which is a bit rich coming from a college student whose prose is tortured by quasi-Marxist twaddle.

Later, as first lady, Hillary possessed the power to act on her contempt for Moynihan, and she threatened to use her power against him if he crossed her. "He's not one of us," a White House aide told *Time* magazine as Hillary was gearing up, in the first week of the Clinton administration, to impose national health care on Capitol Hill. "[W]e'll roll right over him."[4]

In fact, it was Moynihan—then the chairman of the Senate Finance Committee—who did all the rolling. He later publicly spelled out his objections to Hillary's health care plan. "If you have fewer doctors you have fewer doctor bills," he told physicians at Columbia University. "But you don't associate it with improving medicine." He called her plan the "deliberate dumbing down of medicine." Worse, he denounced Hillary's method of assembling a vast politburo of secret committees churning out indescribable proposals: "Working in secret, [is] an abomination where science is concerned and [is] no less an offense to democratic governance."[5]

Such moments of candor reveal that Moynihan was many things that Hillary Rodham Clinton will never be.

He was a singular figure in twentieth-century American politics—not just a Fulbright scholar and Harvard professor, but a genuine match in erudition, wit, and knowledge for all the past giants of the Senate.

He was also self-made. A one-time shoeshine boy from Hell's Kitchen, Moynihan rose to national attention by dint of his imagination and ability. He served four presidents. He did not dart in and out of countries as a casual visitor to lecture his hosts and snatch a few photo ops. He was an accomplished diplomat who served as United States ambassador to India and to the United Nations.

In the Senate he was an active politician, ready to wheel and deal with the rest of them on bridges and highways. Yet he was a man of great intellectual achievement, ranging beyond daily politics. He was a genuine intellectual, and something more. Moynihan was famously indifferent to political caution. Truth mattered to him.

As ambassador to the United Nations, he did not shrink from calling Idi Amin "a racist murderer." After a General Assembly resolution equated Zionism with racism, he said, "The United States rises to declare before the General Assembly of the United Nations, and before the world that it does not acknowledge, it will not abide by, and it will never acquiesce in this infamous act."

It is difficult to imagine any of Moynihan's contemporaries in either party speaking with such Churchillian defiance, and when he did so speak he was speaking as the representative of a Republican administration. He served as President Gerald Ford's ambassador to the United Nations, having been asked years before to take the post by President Richard Nixon, in whose White House he was then serving. In *A Dangerous Place,* the illuminating book Moynihan wrote about his historic service at the United Nations during the Cold War, he noted something in Nixon that reveals the magnanimity and perceptiveness of his own mind: "Nixon understood more about liberals than liberals ever understood about him. He took it as given that we [liberals such as Moynihan] had a role in the scheme of things—a tolerance not always reciprocated."[6]

Moynihan was not only sufficiently public-spirited to serve both parties at the highest level, he was also sufficiently free of partisanship to be prescient in a way Hillary is not. She talks about the future—and everything else—only in ways that maximize her political advantage. Moynihan made fearless predictions, even when they were politically inconvenient or ideologically troublesome.

A liberal Democrat—never a leftist—he opened himself to considerable abuse in the heated days of civil rights for predicting the breakup of the black family owing to paternalistic government. In 1980, he was among the first to write about the coming dissolution of the Soviet Union. At the time, liberal orthodoxy held that the Soviet Union was eternal—hence the need for peaceful coexistence and arms control. He offended bleeding-heart liberals everywhere by anticipating the successful crime-fighting approach of New York City mayor Rudy Giuliani, in which crackdowns on relatively minor street crimes like graffiti would go a long way in restoring law and order.

These unorthodoxies led many to label him a neoconservative. For a time in the 1970s he was. I knew him very well. He was one of the inspirations for a little band of intellectuals then leaving the liberal side for the conservative side. People such as Irving Kristol and Norman Podhoretz (to whom *A Dangerous Place* is dedicated), Midge Decter, and Jeane Kirkpatrick, believed liberal politics was becoming utopian, ignoring threats then rampant against American security and against democracy worldwide. We attended conferences and social gatherings together. Moynihan was one of us. He was an authentic post–World War II liberal who, as Nixon's urban affairs adviser, counseled the president on much of the big government domestic agenda of the Nixon White House. He shared with Nixon a disgust over the radical left-wing ideology that was supplanting liberalism at the core of the Democratic Party, and was alarmed by the McGovern takeover of the party.

Liberalism was turning radical, he said, because of its propensity to wish "so many things so, [that] we all too readily come to think them not only possible, which they very likely are, but also near at hand, which is seldom the case," he wrote. This strain of excessive optimistic bred a "can't wait" tendency in the liberal mind, which in turn made it intolerant of uncomfortable truths and bothersome facts. He concluded: "Liberalism faltered when it turned out it could not cope with truth."[7]

The leftism that Moynihan opposed has remained revealed truth to Hillary Rodham Clinton. This form of liberalism cannot abide contradiction or complexity. As a result of its inability to accept contradictory truths, Moynihan realized that modern liberalism assumed "the ability to immediately dissolve every statement of fact into a question of motive."[8] Historian Steven F. Hayward observes that this tendency, more than anything else, had led to the practice of what the Clintons call the "politics of personal destruction." The Clintons attribute it to Republicans, but their record reveals them as early practitioners.

Moynihan's devotion to truth was to be expected in a man schooled in the classical tradition. He followed the facts as he saw them. His reading eventually led him away from the neocons, and when he left we missed him. It was, however, a political break based on intellectual integrity. I still cherish a silver cup that he sent me from India on the occasion of the birth of my son, Patrick, inscribed, "To Patrick Daniel Tyrrell from Daniel Patrick Moynihan." It is evidence of the politically polluted nature of the *Kultursmog* enshrouding us that when Pat died no major news organization recorded the nearly two decades during which he was a neocon fellow traveler.

This kind of refurbishing of history suits the tradition favored by Hillary. She picked it up from her intellectual mentor, Saul Alinsky, who derided the intellectual commitment to objective truth that was a hallmark of Pat's life. The radical, Alinsky wrote, "knows that all values are relative, in a world of political relativity."[9] For the radical, truth is a tool, infinitely malleable, and what matters is not truth, but symbols.

Pat Moynihan was a despised symbol among American leftists for most of his life. Then he became a useful tool. As he drifted back to the left and age sapped his independence, a heartfelt commitment to party loyalty allowed him to swallow any misgivings he might have had about Madame Hillary taking his seat in the Senate. In death, Pat has become another emblem of endorsement to slap on the side of her bandwagon. But the record as found in his writings and the part of his life the obituaries left out makes clear, Daniel Patrick Moynihan was not Hillary's kind of liberal.

In her memoirs, Hillary assures us that in 2002 she dug up her old college thesis and ran it by the former senator, who—ever the professor—marked it up and returned it with an "A." She also reports that he scribbled a commentary. She does not say what he scribbled.[10]

Coat and Tie Radicals vs. Penny-Loafer Conservatives

In positioning herself for the looming intergenerational battle against the Bushies and their fellow 1960s conservatives, Hillary is still sustained by the left-wing texts that sent her and other Coat and Tie Radicals to the barricades in the first place. Their texts are fundamentally different from those that sustained the young conservatives of the 1960s. The conservatives' texts varied in intellectual terms, for with thirty years' hindsight we can see that the young conservatives were by disposition and by intellect a more diverse lot than students on the left. George W. Bush's text seems to have been *Esquire's Handbook for Hosts*. His more ideologically developed conservative classmates read longer books by Russell Kirk and Milton Friedman. Kirk described how "eternal verities" sustained a free society. Friedman, most notably in *Capitalism and Freedom*, critiqued paternalistic government and suggested governmental reforms, for instance educational vouchers. These were books about the principles of Western civilization.

As for the Coat and Tie Radicals, after reading condensations of Marx and Engels for fury and utopia, Martin Heidegger and Herbert Marcuse for despising their bourgeois origins, they turned to manuals instructing them how to create utopia and how to stomp on most Western values. *Rules for Radicals* by Saul Alinsky was the left-wingers' operating manual for revolution. Hillary was one of the book's most gullible readers.

From Alinsky she derived three rules that sustain her to this very day, which will assist her in sending the Bushies to the guillotine or to an early retirement home, all depending on who her attorney general might be. Hillary's First Rule of Politics is: In the struggle for power, tactics take precedence over principles. As *Rules for Radicals* puts it, "Ethical standards must be elastic to stretch with the times."[11] If ordinary Americans are not fully cognizant of how Hillary has stretched ethical standards, several prosecutors are.

Hillary's Second Rule: Confrontation is a gift. It clears the way to demonize opponents, energize supporters, and overtake enemy ground, thereby enlarging the kingdom. Alinsky writes, "Pick the target, freeze it, personalize it, and polarize it."[12] Polarize it? What the Clintons identified in the 1990s as the "politics of personal destruction," which they cleverly attributed to the Republicans, they learned from Alinsky and implemented for three decades against political opponents, journalists, and women who might snitch on Bill.

Hillary's Third Rule: The continuous struggle to win brings meaning to one's life. Again, the *locus classicus* is found in *Rules for Radicals*: "Knowing that the mountain has no top, that it is a perpetual quest from plateau to plateau, the question arises, 'Why the struggle, the conflict, the heartbreak, the danger, the sacrifice? Why the constant climb?' Our answer is the same as that which a real mountain climber gives when he is asked why he does what he does. 'Because it's there.'"[13]

Washington pundits remarked that Hillary had "deepened" and was displaying a new level of maturity, or worse, "spirituality," after she invoked existential themes in an April 7, 1993, address to students at the University of Texas at Austin. The first lady spoke of a "crisis of meaning" and a "spiritual vacuum" besetting the country. She told her Texas audience that "remolding society" is the great challenge of the West and that the only way to overcome this was to address the "lack of meaning" in American life. Once Americans had addressed their meaningless lives, Hillary was at hand with the solution: "We need a

new politics of meaning. We need a new ethos of individual respon-
sibility and caring" to "fill that spiritual vacuum."

Reporters should not have been surprised. Truth be known, this
speech is not unlike many public utterances Hillary had made during
her college days and immediately thereafter when she was still effer-
vescent with radical bilge. There is the jabber about "meaning," the
utter absorption with politics, and, as close students of Hillary will
also detect, the residual influence of Alinsky. Lineaments of the Three
Rules that he inspired in her stand out in the Texas speech. Confrontation is recommended. "Ethical standards" have been stretched
to harmonize with changing times. A "new politics of meaning," offers
power, especially to those who master those new politics. At the University of Texas, Hillary even identified an opponent to demonize, the
recently deceased Republican political operative Lee Atwater, the first
President Bush's Dick Morris.

As she was to do later in *Living History*, Hillary, in her "Politics of
Meaning" speech, gratuitously appropriated the gloomy musings
Atwater had written on his deathbed. Dying from brain cancer, he had
penned a wistful piece for *Life* magazine in which he expressed regret
that ambition had monopolized his life, leaving it devoid of the deeper
things, which for him were "a little more time with my family" or "an
evening with my friends." Hillary pounces on this admission. Rather
than admitting to any failure in her own apparently exemplary life,
she exploits the regrets of a dead Republican, identifying the deceased
with ruthlessness, selfishness, and ambition. As Alinsky prescribed,
Hillary picked the target, froze it, and personalized it. To the assembled University of Texas students, she concluded, "Who will lead us
out of this spiritual vacuum?" The question, of course, answers itself:
Hillary and Bill.

Hillary's opponents and apologists alike attributed this speech to the influence of Michael Lerner, the writer who popularized the phrase "Politics of Meaning" in his journal of far-left sugar plumbs, *Tikkun,* and in a book by the same title. The writings of Lerner are not simply leftist, they are almost Dadaist in their absurdity, often railing against patriarchy, homophobia, and that *dreaded* "tyranny of couples." Lerner and his first wife exchanged wedding rings constructed from metal taken from downed U.S. military aircraft. They had "Smash Monogamy" inscribed on their wedding cake.[14]

Briefly, in the spring of 1993, Hillary was breathless in her enthusiasm for Lerner. Madame Hillary instinctively apprehended the usefulness of his didactic pontifications on new ways of *thinking* and *feeling.* Madame Hillary is herself a case study of what psychiatrists call "the controlling personality," and such personalities are forever on the lookout for more efficient techniques of control. Her seemingly gratuitous lies have served, as I noted earlier, to control those conditions around her, or at least to reassure her that she is in control of conditions around her. In 1993, with her health care plans unraveling, she was a controlling personality in greater need of reassurance than ever before. Whether jackass or gift horse, Lerner's august flapdoodle would leave even large audiences speechless in the palm of her hand, at least until her back was turned and the whistles and laughter began. She would sweep into interviews and public meetings announcing, "As Michael Lerner and I discussed, we have to first create a language that would better communicate what we are trying to say, and the policies would flow from that language."[15]

This was 1960s nonsense on stilts. It could not last long in the 1990s. At the end of May, Michael Kelly wrote a derisive peace in the *New York Times Magazine,* "Saint Hillary." Hillary soon sensed that members of the press shared Kelly's amusement over her relationship with Lerner, and she executed a move that she performs flawlessly, as Vince Foster learned during his brief and unhappy period at the White House. She dropped Lerner, never mentioning him again as an influence on her or even as a fond memory. In *Living History*, Lerner should appear between "Leno, Jay" and "Letterman, David," perhaps with the explanation reference: "Lerner, Michael; speech, University of Texas." There is nothing. To friends, she confided that he had used her, precisely the opposite of the way relationships are supposed to be experienced by Madame Hillary.

Lerner survived his relationship with Hillary and continued on as a New Age huckster in venues less august than 1600 Pennsylvania Avenue. Foster's fall from favor was more tragic. To this day, there is not much consensus on the cause of his suicide in a park overlooking Washington, but there should be no doubt about the strong sentiments that once existed between him and Hillary. Dick Morris speaks of how Hillary was hurt by her husband's infidelities from the earliest stages of their marriage (Morris says she is over the hurt now and that the Clintons' present relationship is simply business, the business being politics)[16] and continuing on through their tenure in the Arkansas governor's mansion. Becky Brown, a nanny for the Clintons in those days, has spoken on the record of how Hillary would petulantly discuss her marriage with Brown as well as her contempt for Foster's wife, who, she claimed, was "so damned jealous." "I don't know why Vince stays with her," Hillary told the nanny. Brown's husband, a favorite bodyguard of the Clintons in the mid-1980s, has testified to seeing Hillary and Foster exchanging intimacies, and other state troopers are on record claiming to have seen similar behavior. They claim that Foster would stay with Hillary at the governor's mansion "into the wee hours of the morning" when Governor Clinton was gone, and that they saw public caressing. At least two troopers drove Foster and Hillary to a Rose Law Firm mountain retreat in Heber Springs, Arkansas, for trysts. Even Hillary's former law partner, disgraced associate attorney general Webb Hubbell, makes it clear in his memoir, *Friends in High Places*, that the relationship between Foster and Hillary was unusually close. Yet the closeness ended when Hillary became dissatisfied with Foster's work as deputy White House counsel, and after his tragic death he was simply another Lerner in her life, a has-been.[17]

Hillary's Lerner interlude has led many observers to conclude that the first lady was passing through a new phase (having been made vulnerable by the lingering illness and death of her father), in which she allowed herself to get carried away. However, as we have seen, Hillary was not going through a new phase. This was just Madame Hillary popping up again, the controlling personality, the self-promoting dynamo, the self-regarding existentialist.

People who want to "remold" society are, by definition, radical; radicals alarm a modern electorate. (Or, to employ Hillary's definition from her undergraduate thesis that examined the Alinskyian approach to poverty programs, "A radical is one who advocates sweeping changes in the existing laws and methods of government. These proposed changes are aimed at the roots of political problems which in Marxian terms are the attitudes and the behaviors of men." Yes, young Hillary took "Marxian terms" seriously.) Radicals are also, by definition, arrogant; arrogant public figures anger the modern electorate. For the good of Senator Clinton's future, she must keep this radicalism and arrogance in check. People who know her, for instance, Dick Morris, tell me the New Hillary has matured. She is no longer the angry youth of the 1960s or the angry first lady of the Clinton scandals. Time will tell. Talk of a New Hillary brings to mind talk, in the mid-1960s, of a New Nixon, who, as noted, shared certain weaknesses with Hillary. Just as there never really was a New Nixon, sources in the Senate insist Senator Clinton's dominant desire is to "beat Republicans."

In adopting Alinsky's *Rules for Radicals,* the youthful Hillary was giving herself over to a political value that is the unchanging essence of all progressives, liberal and radical alike: that misdemeanor of disturbing the peace. By seeking to disturb the peace through politics rather than through the unruly conduct characteristic of most misdemeanants (say, breaking beer bottles on the sidewalk or kicking over garbage cans), Hillary has avoided jail and bathed herself in the applause of various interest groups in the Democratic Party. She has also managed to attain her deepest ambition in life, attracting attention. Alinsky too was, *au fond,* an attention seeker, as he innocently reveals in the above dithyramb about topless mountains and endless hill climbs. Hillary is entoiled with politics because it has always favored her with nigh on limitless public attention.

One of the failings of her political life—and it is a failing that Alinsky's existential vaporings only encouraged—is that thus far she has not accomplished much in politics, other than getting herself and her husband elected to high office. As Morris has observed in his informative book about life in the Clinton administration, *Behind the Oval Office: Getting Reelected Against All Odds*, eight years in the White House saw few policies implemented. Clinton was, Morris said famously, a one-term president who served eight years. A flurry of presidential initiatives passed in 1995 and 1996, for instance, the welfare reform bill and a budget deal. All came after Clinton, having lost Congress and many state offices for the Democrats, brought Morris in to win the next election, a rescue mission Morris had performed for the Clintons back in 1982 after Hillary's leftist extravagances had cost her husband the governorship. (The same barren legislative record can be seen during the Clinton governorships.)

This lack of a legislative record could arguably benefit the New Hillary, for what legislation she has attempted as Bill's partner in politics has almost always been far left and repugnant to the electorate. Even as Senator Clinton she has achieved little in legislative terms, which, to be fair, is par for the course for a freshman senator. Her prodigality is mainly in attaching her name to the bills sponsored by other powerful members of Congress, especially Republicans. What she is also good at—and the Senate a perfect forum for—is, once again, disturbing the peace.

That the Clintons' incessant politicking would lead to exiguous policy achievements might surprise those Americans who hold the popular belief that the Clintons are political geniuses. Yet a careful reading of Alinsky's *Rules* and a modicum of thought about Hillary's derivative Three Rules reveal no program of ideological imperatives and no objective goals other than endless "opposition," "perpetual quests," "spiritual vacuums," and contemplation of the meaning of "meaning." This is more 1960s nonsense, propped up by little more than youthful arrogance. No serious politician has to search very far for meaning in politics. Most find plenty of meaning in delivering the pork or slowing government growth, providing for the security of the nation or putting a smile on a constituent's face. Yet for years Hillary has given herself over to The Immensities as adumbrated by such swamis as Alinsky and Lerner. Consider one of her earliest recorded outbursts, her famous 1969 student commencement address at Wellesley.

Edward Brooke, a liberal Republican and the first African-American elected to the Senate since Reconstruction, had preceded her on the podium to say, "Whatever the romantics may say about violence in our national life, the use of force is repugnant to the spirit of American politics." This was not the kind of exhortation the radicals of the Class of '69 expected. To their ears, accustomed as they were to their professors' lectures on alienation and protest, this liberal Republican might as well have been Spiro T. Agnew or Joseph R. McCarthy.

Hillary and her contemporaries had forced the college administration to clear a place for her on the podium by threatening to hold a counter-graduation protest. Hillary took the podium to castigate the bewildered Brooke, saying *á la* Alinsky "We're searching for more immediate, ecstatic and penetrating modes of living." Ecstatic? Penetrating? Now we know what young Bill Clinton saw behind the Coke-bottle lenses of Hillary's granny glasses. "Every protest," the young spellbinder went on, "every dissent, whether it's an individual academic paper, Founder's parking lot demonstration, [!] is unabashedly an attempt to forge an identity in this particular age."[18]

From college days to first lady days, the quest continues. In her youth it has its lewd suggestions of the "ecstatic." In middle age the quest encounters "crisis." Throughout, the talk is of "politics" pursuant to "meaning" and even "identity." Most successful politicians settle on their identity before they seek public office. Abraham Lincoln knew who he was—a backwoodsman who, by dint of intelligence and wit, had become a razor-sharp lawyer. Franklin D. Roosevelt knew who he was—an upper-class gentleman who willed himself to rise from his sickbed to attain the presidency. In Bill and Hillary Clinton, we see two people for whom power-seeking began at adolescence, when most people are still trying to sort out who they are and who they will become. Hillary seems not to understand that in speaking of her career in such narcissistic terms, she is implicitly admitting that without the klieg lights and applause, she would have no identity. When I asked Morris about the adult Hillary's private life, he responded, "I don't think she's had one." With a look back on the statements she has made through the decades, it is clear that without power, she would be, literally, a nobody—to borrow a phrase from Walker Percy—a ghost in the cosmos.

Saul Alinsky

To understand how Hillary came to embrace the Three Rules that have governed her life, it is necessary to step back from the smooth prevarications of her memoir and study Hillary's real biography, the ideological development of a public person with little else in her life. She grew up in the middle-class Chicago suburb of Park Ridge, the daughter of an unhappy mother practicing a traditional 1950s motherhood and an acerbic, somewhat bumptious father, a small-time capitalist and owner of a plant that manufactured fabrics. Hillary went to Wellesley and Yale Law School, growing ever more the 1960s radical, so her ideological biography is even more important than the chronological details.

Many figures have influenced Hillary Rodham Clinton, but radical activist Saul Alinsky stands before all the others. Blunt and acidulous, learned and street-smart, alternately charming and vulgar, Alinsky was the archetypal professional radical. Born in the slums of Chicago in 1909, he studied criminology at the University of Chicago, where his interests in graduate school led him to perform a detached study of the political economy of Al Capone and his organization.

In the 1930s, Alinsky gave up academics for a lifelong avocation of organizing the poor and oppressed. He studied labor organization from the venerable John L. Lewis of the United Mine Workers Union, adapting what he learned to forge his own unique philosophy and method. "Alinsky outlines American history focusing on men he would call 'radical,' confronting his readers again with the 'unique' way Americans have synthesized the alien roots of radicalism, Marxism, Utopian socialism, syndicalism, the French Revolution, with their own conditions and experiences," Hillary wrote in her undergraduate thesis.

In time, Alinsky came to believe that the traditional labor method of confrontation and negotiation was insufficient. The only thing that could transform social conditions was to organize the oppressed and engage in bruising confrontations to wrest power from the oppressors. "Power is the very essence, the dynamo of life," Alinsky would later write. "It is the power of the heart pumping blood and sustaining life in the body. It is the power of active citizen participation pulsing upward, providing a unified strength for a common purpose."[19]

Alinsky turned his attention to Chicago's infamous Back of the Yards area, the very neighborhood dramatized earlier in the century by Upton Sinclair in *The Jungle*. Alinsky successfully organized this impoverished community against the meatpacking industry and its friends in City Hall. In the 1950s and 1960s he adapted his methods to confront Eastman Kodak over the plight of the black ghetto in Rochester, New York, and indoctrinated people as disparate as Dick Morris, Caesar Chavez, and, of course, one undergraduate student-government type at Wellesley.

Alinsky divided society into three classes, the Haves, the Have-Nots, and the middle class, which he called the Have-a-Little, Want Mores. Just as Machiavelli's *The Prince* instructed the Haves on how to retain power, so Alinsky set out in two books, *Reveille for Radicals* (1947) and the far more influential *Rules for Radicals* (1971) to instruct radical organizers in how to advance the interests of the Have-Nots.

In his writings, Alinsky revels in an explicit nihilism that respects and wants nothing but power for its own sake. "An organizer working in and for an open society is in an ideological dilemma," he wrote. "To begin with, he does not have a fixed truth—truth to him is relative and changing, *everything* to him is relative and changing. He is a political relativist."[20] In a world without fixed principles, it is necessary to dispense with artificial and constricting concepts like morality or fairness. "It is a world not of angels but of angles, where men speak of moral principles but act on power principles; a world where we are always moral and our enemies always immoral; a world where 'reconciliation' means that when one side gets the power and the other side gets reconciled to it, then we have reconciliation...."[21]

He writes of an attempt to involve him in sexual blackmail against a corporate opponent who was a closet homosexual. Alinsky turned down this proposal, but made it clear it was only for tactical reasons: "...if I had been convinced that the only way we could win was to use it, then without any reservations I would have used it. What was my alternative? To draw myself into righteous 'moral' indignation, saying, 'I would rather lose than corrupt my principles,' than go home with my ethical hymen intact?"[22] Alinsky believed that the "real arena is corrupt and bloody. Life is a corrupting process from the time a child learns to play his mother off against his father in the politics of when to go to bed; he who fears corruption fears life."[23] Hillary and her fellow Coat and Tie Radicals probably absorbed the amorality that came to characterize their lives from many sources, but Alinsky was surely a major one. In a rare effort at concision, he wrote, "The means-and-ends moralists or non-doers always wind up on their ends without any means."[24] Those who are perplexed that so soon after reveling in the idealism of Yale Law School Hillary would participate in her sleazy cattle futures deal in Arkansas might find that $100,000 payoff more comprehensible if they were aware of these passages from Alinsky, especially where he writes that "the real arena is corrupt." From Marx to Alinsky, many of the Clintons' mentors have denied the legitimacy of the American polity, so why not take it for a few bucks?

While Alinsky's is a recipe for endlessly disturbing the peace and rendering society an anarchistic stew, the sage himself was no Robespierre. He denounced the Weathermen for taking the "grand cop-out, suicide."[25] He reminded 1960s radicals that they enjoyed rights to protest that would never have been permitted in Havana, Moscow, or Beijing. He even admonished them not to call police "pigs" or "motherfuckers," because such language is offensive to the lower middle class, the very people to be rescued from their misguided respect for the establishment.

"I agreed with some of Alinsky's ideas," Senator Hillary Clinton writes in *Living History*. "But we had a fundamental disagreement. He believed you could change the system only from the outside. I didn't."[26] Middle-aged and facing the electorate in an era vastly more conservative than the America of her college days, Hillary the memoirist has good reason to distance herself from Alinsky. Still, it would have been wiser just to ignore him as she ignored Michael Lerner. Instead, as she does so often in *Living History*, she lays down a lie that is easily refuted. A review of Alinsky's life and writings simply does not support the idea that he would have disapproved of an attempt to change (really, subvert) the system from within.

In 1968, a year before Hillary's thesis, Alinsky waded into the tear-gas and mayhem that surrounded the Democratic convention. He met with students who had followed Eugene McCarthy in the New Hampshire Democratic primary, then Robert F. Kennedy, only to see their dream ended by a bullet in the kitchen of the Ambassador Hotel. They confronted Alinsky, many of them still, perhaps, bruised from recent demonstrations. "Mr. Alinsky, we fought in primary after primary and the people voted *no* on Vietnam. Look at that convention. They're not paying any attention to the vote. Look at your police and the army. You still want us to work in the system?"[27]

Alinsky was characteristically blunt to the young radicals (one of them could have been Hillary—she and her good friend Betsy Johnson had run off for the demonstrations at Grant Park the moment they saw the chaos on television.)[28] Alinsky told them they had three choices. "One, go find a wailing wall and feel sorry for yourselves. Two, go psycho and start bombing—but this will only swing people to the right. Three, learn a lesson. Go home, organize, build power and at the next convention, *you be the delegates.*"[29]

As early as May 1967—two years before Hillary's undergraduate thesis and her supposed break with Alinsky—the old radical was pioneering the use of corporate proxies by persuading the National Unitarian Convention to join the struggle against Eastman Kodak. It was Alinsky who thought up the idea—now commonplace—to use proxies to harass management from within.

Hillary has to know this. It is wrong—in the extreme—to portray Alinsky as a man who thought change could come only from outside agitation. He was often hunting for ways to get inside an organization, always probing for cracks and opportunities to change it from within. Though he always spoke of his opposition as "the enemy," he extolled compromise as a key tactic in the organizer's manual. A man who tells student radicals to become convention delegates is not averse to changing the system from within. It is obvious, however, why Hillary would want to distance herself from Alinsky. The Alinsky connection comes too close to revealing Madame Hillary. Moreover, in an era when capitalism and globalism are practiced almost everywhere, with socialism forced to hide behind a "Third Way" facade, an ambitious politician might admit to admiring Alinsky's idealism but never his politics.

From Methodism to Maoism

As we have seen, a compulsive ambition has driven Hillary since an early age. Perhaps it is the consequence of suffering a stern and demanding father. (Interestingly, over the years she has expressed an intensifying resentment to her "Father-Knows-Best upbringing.")[30] It is possibly a trait she actually inherited from the hardworking Chicago businessman. Her appetite for power is traceable throughout her early life, in the oft-told tales of young Hillary, her writing NASA at age fourteen expressing the desire to be an astronaut, her first defeats and victories in student government, her rise as an honor student.[31]

Other character traits were obvious at an early age. Hillary Rodham graduated in the top five percent of her high school and was voted by her classmates as "most likely to succeed." Yet she probably was not going to succeed on the merits of her personality. Hillary's high school classmates also joked that she might become a nun, dubbing her "Sister Frigidaire."

Hillary coyly spins these stereotypes in favorable ways. She likes to dwell on the fact that she was once a Goldwater girl, complete with AuH20 emblazoned on her cowboy hat; that she read Goldwater's *Conscience of a Conservative*; and worked as an intern for the House Republican Conference. (It is amusing to see her photographed as an

AFP/CORBIS

▲▼ Long the power behind the throne, Hillary has now reversed those roles.

Reuters NewMedia Inc./CORBIS

▲ Madame Hillary is keeping her eyes on the opposition, one of whom is more dangerous than the rest.

◀ Senator Hillary's first challenge was taking control of New York, and her target was Senator Chuck Schumer.

▲ Democratic wheelhorses: the older generation eyes the new generation.

▲ Senator Daniel Patrick Moynihan and Senator-elect Hillary Rodham Clinton: divided by a deep animosity only a few remember.

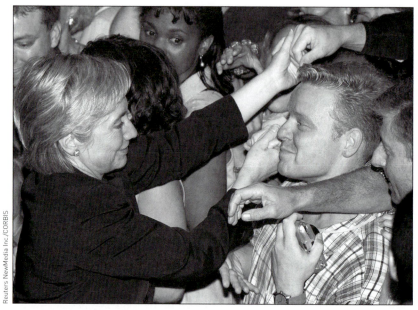

▲ Campaigning for her Senate seat, Hillary had to overcome the traits she shared with Richard M. Nixon, her prey from 1974.

▲ Campaigning against George W. Bush, the Clintons represent 1960s Coat and Tie Radicals' last hope to speak for their generation.

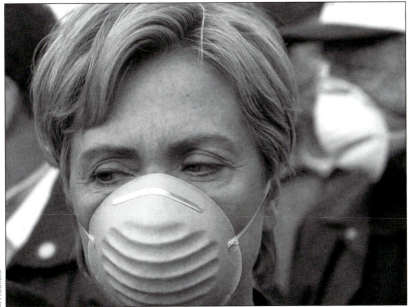

▲ One way to protect from the *Kultursmog*. (see Chapter Two)

◀ Commander-in-chief? When?

The Woman of Many Hairdos…

▲ The authoress of the "Vast Right-Wing Conspiracy" with her Richard Mellon Soros.

◀ What's to stop Madame Hillary?

intern in front of the Capitol with Congressman Gerald Ford. Will history someday record both the lumbering congressman and the girl with the eager-beaver smile as occupants of the Oval Office? Times change.)

In *Living History*, Hillary sourly recalls the triumph of Richard Nixon and the gradual disappearance of the Rockefeller wing of the Republican Party. "I sometimes think that I didn't leave the Republican Party as much as it left me," she writes, lifting Ronald Reagan's famous line about his departure from the Democratic Party without even a facetious attribution to the fortieth president.[32] Not surprisingly, Reagan's statement reflected the genuine experience of his life, while Hillary followed her own bent ever further to the left, far beyond the country club Republicanism of Rockefeller. The Republican Party has remained Goldwaterite for decades, and those Goldwater roots go back to Republican conservatives such as Senator Robert Taft in the late 1930s and before that to Calvin Coolidge. The Democratic Party has changed more radically than the Republicans, being today almost nothing like the muscular party of Franklin Roosevelt and Harry Truman. The Coat and Tie Radicals squalling at Vice President Hubert Humphrey and Mayor Richard J. Daley at the 1968 Democratic convention *are* the delegates now, which explains why the nomination is Hillary's whenever she wants it. The Democratic Party's weakness for Alinsky's amoral cynicism and ceaseless politicizing has cost them their position as the country's majority party.

Hillary's drift leftward from Goldwater to Rockefeller to Alinsky can be traced back to the Rev. Don Jones, an earnest thirty-year-old theologian at Park Ridge's First Methodist Church. Hillary was in the ninth grade when Jones introduced her to World Council of Churches liberalism in his "University of Life" classes at First Methodist. From

Jones, Hillary learned some of the precepts that would later form the basis of her personal ideology.

It is essential at this point to understand that Methodism was not just an acceptable Protestant domination casually adopted by the suburban Rodham family. Hillary's father knelt by his bed every evening to pray.[33] In *It Takes a Village*, Hillary recounted, "We talked with God, walked with God, ate, studied and argued with God."[34] A certain amount of do-goodism goes along with the Methodist creed. Hillary would, of course, have often heard John Wesley's admonition to "Do all the good you can, by all the means you can, in all the ways you can, in all the places you can, at all the times you can, to all the people you can, as long as ever you can." Though her father was a conservative, Hillary would become steeped in the Methodist tradition of the Social Gospel, shaped as it was by a benevolent socialism and scientific positivism. Goldwater's scruples about the Founding Fathers' reverence for limited government were ultimately lost on her.

Through Jones, Hillary came to know the thinking of the German-American existential theologian Paul Tillich, who adapted Christian thinking to the then–dominant intellectual currents of Marxism and existentialism. Tillich, however, redefined the classical Marxist problem of man's alienation, casting it in wider, spiritual terms. It is here—decades before meeting Michael Lerner—that Hillary came to hear of the modern crisis of meaning, and came to dwell on her persistent themes of finding some way to restore meaning to modern life. Where Tillich, however, redirected alienated man to seek meaning in communion with Christ, Hillary would come to seek existential meaning in the continuous pursuit of power. "My sense of Hillary," Jones would later tell the late Michael Kelly, "is that she realizes absolutely the truth of the human condition, which is that you cannot depend on the basic nature of man to be good and you cannot depend entirely on moral suasion to make it good. You have to use power. And there is nothing wrong with wielding power in the pursuit of policies that will add to the human good. I think Hillary knows this. She is very much the sort of Christian who understands that the use of power to achieve social good is legitimate."[35]

Don Jones broke the conservative cocoon of Hillary's suburban life, taking her to hear Martin Luther King, Jr.'s lecture "Remaining Awake Through a Revolution," and to shake hands with the man himself. It was Jones who brought this child of suburban comfort into contact with people from the inner city and the world of migrant laborers. Her exposure deepened from favoring civil rights in high school to radicalism in college. One milestone on this journey was Hillary's discovery of *Motive*, a Methodist magazine for young adults. As first lady, Hillary told *Newsweek* that she kept every back issue of *Motive*. She also told *Newsweek* of her special admiration of a piece by Carl Oglesby, "Change or Containment," crediting it with shaking up her thinking on the Vietnam War.[36]

The presence of a man of Oglesby's radicalism in the pages of this Methodist magazine reveals how alienated from middle-class America at least some editors and readers at *Motive* had become. Hillary did not remind her *Newsweek* interviewer that Oglesby was a Maoist and a one-time president of Students for a Democratic Society. Nor did she dwell on Oglesby's defenses of Castro and Ho Chi Minh or mention his approval of revolutionary violence.

At Wellesley, Hillary encountered a secular do-goodism that, like the Social Gospel do-goodism of the Methodist Church, became infiltrated and subverted by the left. The school motto, "not to be served, but to serve," has the Wesleyan ring of goodwill, and the same understated *noblesse oblige*. It was at Wellesley, of course, that Hillary completed the political metamorphosis that had begun with Goldwater, moved to Rockefeller, continued on to more liberal Republicans, such as New York mayor John Lindsay, and finally crossed over into the Democratic camp, with vociferous support of first Eugene McCarthy's presidential campaign and then that of Robert F. Kennedy. With the increased turbulence of the late 1960s, her ideological journey took her much further, though, beyond Kennedy and into the hard left—into the company of the Black Panthers and their apologists.

By the time Hillary arrived at Yale Law School, she was already a rising star of the 1960s generation, profiled in *Life* magazine (along with a young activist from Brown, Ira Magaziner, who would join her in the White House in 1993 to ride her health care death wagon), and renowned for her leadership in winning the College Bowl quiz show. She accepted as mentors people such as Charles Garry, the radical lawyer who defended the Black Panthers despite their persistent calls for police assassinations. She approved when spineless administrators at Yale allowed radical organizers to take over the campus, disrupting scholarship and studies. Hillary actually organized students to monitor the local trial of Black Panthers accused of torturing a police informant to death. The informant's name was Alex Rackley, and while the country's *Kultursmog* keeps the tragedies of Kent State and Grant Park enshrined in glory along with such other radical legal proceedings as the trial of the Chicago Eight, the sufferings of citizens such as Rackley at the hands of leftist radicals go unremembered. He was beaten, scalded, and mutilated before being killed. Hillary took his tormentors' side.

In *Living History*, Hillary records the story of a Yale professor who had been a refugee from Nazi Germany. Hillary approached him in tears over the deaths at Kent State. "I told him I couldn't believe what was happening; he chilled me by saying that, for him, it was all too familiar."[37] It apparently never occurs to Hillary that the depravities practiced by the Black Panthers on the East Coast and the heavy hand of the Orwellian "free speech movement" on the West Coast were more redolent of the Beer Hall Putsch than a few panicked National Guardsmen with live ammunition.

As a law student, Hillary eschewed the law journal to serve on the board of editors of the *Yale Review of Law and Social Action*. Serving alongside Mickey Kantor and Robert Reich (two more Coat and Tie Radicals who would serve in the Clinton administration), she was part of an editorial board that published angry anti-American writing by radical lawyers such as Charles Garry and William Kuntsler and infantile incivism by the Yippie practitioner of guerrilla theater Jerry Rubin, who exhorted parents to "to get high with our seven-year-olds" and to "kill our parents."[38] (Rubin became a successful businessman of sorts in the 1980s, and died after a jay-walking accident in 1994, a violent death but not the kind of violent death one might have foreseen for him in 1972.)

As an associate editor of the fall/winter issue of 1970, Hillary oversaw the production of articles on Bobby Seale and the Black Panther trials (one of which would tie up New Haven in protests). Cartoons depicted the police as pigs muttering "niggers, niggers, niggers, niggers." Another cartoon in this supposedly serious law review depicted a police officer as a decapitated and eviscerated pig. It was under Hillary's authority that another article appeared, "Jamestown 70," by James Blumstein and James Phelan, which argued for mass hippie migration to a single American state that the migrants could then transform into a "living laboratory." (Does that explain the transformation of contemporary Vermont into a laboratory of liber-alism, and the sudden emergence of Dr. Howard Dean in 2003 as a promising Democratic presidential candidate, the Ben and Jerry's political flavor of the month?) Read from the perspective of the twenty-first century, "Jamestown 70," is charmingly naïve in its Rousseauean raptures. But it is here that we first encounter echoes of something more sinister: Hillary's insistence that we "remold" society.

As an editor, Hillary kept critiquing the article ("mental mastur-bation" was the popular 1960s radical term she neatly interpolated on the manuscript), always seeking to get the authors to back up their New Consciousness with concrete actions. "Get more specific. Get down to earth," she instructed them.[39]

"While some 1960s radicals on the wilder fringes might have been merely self-indulgent fantasists, or spoiled college kids seeking to avoid the responsibilities of their parents," wrote the late Barbara Olson, "Hillary was a budding Leninist. Menshevik, Bolshevik, Trot-skyite—they were all debating societies. What really mattered to Lenin—and what Saul Alinsky taught Hillary to value—was *power*."[40]

At Yale, in the midst of the demonstrations and the ritual sacking of Eugene Rostow's office, between the long discussions on social change, the Black Panthers, and the coming revolution, some time was actually devoted to the study and appreciation of the law. Even here, however, Marxist thinking had subverted the law's semantic roots. Hillary was one of the followers of Duncan Kennedy, who founded Critical Legal Studies—a.k.a. the Crits—a school that had decon-structed the law much as French philosopher Jacques Derrida had deconstructed literature. To put it simply, Crits believe that legal prin-ciples have no intrinsic meaning, and that they certainly are not fixed in any eternal verities like justice or fairness. Law is simply power transformed into doctrine. Deconstructing the words that make up a contract or a statute reveals the instrumentality of the law in the service of a corrupt power establishment. Thus, the law is a semantic weapon that can be turned around to use on the power structure itself. It is here, in these academic roots, that we can appreciate the mentality of another Yale Law graduate, William Jefferson Clinton, who would later distinguish himself by likely becoming the first English-speaking adult, outside a philosophy course, to question the meaning of "is."

It was at Yale, of course, that Hillary first met Bill, "looking more like a Viking than a Rhodes Scholar."[41] He had long hair and what Hillary assumed a Viking's beard might have looked like. Journalist David Maraniss, in *First in His Class*, a masterful biography about Bill depicting both Clintons, reveals a surprising portrait of the future Clinton at Yale:

> Each student was required to write a paper and read it to the class. Clinton went first. The question his paper addressed was whether the pluralist model of society, with its mix of corporations, regulatory agencies, labor unions, consumer groups, environmentalists, citizen advocates, chambers of commerce, could place enough pressure on corporations to make them responsible. Leftist intellectuals led by Herbert Marcuse believed that the answer was no. The pluralist model was a fraud in the final analysis, Marcuse argued, and freedom and democracy were illusions in the corporate capitalist system.

Greg Craig,[42] who was Rodham's friend and another student in the seminar, remembers Clinton's presentation and how surprised he was by it. Everyone at Yale Law knew that Clinton wanted to be a politician and that he still believed strongly in the system. But "the whole thrust of his paper," Craig thought, was that "the pluralist model just didn't work. He said it didn't work because the money was out of whack. The corporations had all the money and they used it to defend themselves. Bill argued that the system was corrupted."[43]

The 1960s and 1970s abounded with critics lecturing students that "the system was corrupt." The real system that enveloped the Clintons and their generational cohorts was academic, not corporate, and it was intellectually corrupt. It was difficult for Hillary and Bill to avoid the likes of Alinsky, the Rev. Jones, and the Crits, as it was hard for all of us in that era, but somehow these two were susceptible to Marcusian criticism while others were not. Some of it was the consequence of the Coat and Tie Radicals' exploitation of their liberal and radical professors. Some of it came from some deep-seated anger. As we have seen, Madame Hillary has this anger. Bill's dominant traits are ambition and appetite, but not anger.

Another ideological influence in Hillary's past arose from her budding relationship with Marian Wright Edelman. The first black woman to pass the Mississippi bar, Edelman became a career advocate for children's rights. Hillary interned for Edelman's Washington Research Project in the early 1970s, pursued the study of children's issues at the Yale Child Study Center, and heard Anna Freud's lectures on child psychology. Edelman's project later morphed into the Children's Defense Fund, which Hillary served as a lawyer and, later on, as a board member.[44] In those years, Penn Rhodeen, a staff attorney at the New Haven Legal Assistance Association, recounted Hillary's appearance for the press: "[S]he had Gloria Steinem glasses, Gloria Steinem hair, a purple sheepskin jacket, and was driving a purple Gremlin. We hit it off well. She had a strong point of view about kids. I was very struck. When you're that young, you're not thinking about children typically. She had this wonderful passion. I don't quite know how she'd gotten so committed so fast."[45]

A reading of Hillary's writings on children's rights supplies the answer, but note that children's rights is a typical Coat and Tie Radical issue. The ever-exploitative Coat and Tie Radical presents children as puppies in the storefront window of her little shop of horrors. Her agenda is children's "rights," which must be discerned and enforced by radical lawyers prepared to "remodel" society. In Hillary's *Harvard Educational Review* article "Children Under the Law," she gave lawyers the go-ahead to "remodel" the family. It is characteristic of the radicalism of the era. Three decades later, as Senator Clinton, she boldly lies about the article's reach. She complains about the "misinterpretation" of her article in *Living History*. "[C]onservative Republicans like Marilyn Quayle and Pat Buchanan would twist my words to portray me as 'anti-family.' Some commentators actually claimed that I wanted children to be able to sue their parents if they were told to take out the garbage."[46]

In the *Harvard Educational Review* piece, however, Hillary explicitly attacks the belief that families are "private, nonpolitical units." She adds, "Ascribing rights to children will . . . force from the judiciary and the legislature institutional support for the child's point of view." It is hard to imagine where she could be going here without concluding that she is advocating the use of children for ideological ends. Who would advocate for children if not so-called public interest lawyers, liberal busybodies who would make it their business to instruct children in the appropriate grievances? What Hillary is talking about here is using children as instruments to persuade the courts to order sweeping changes in social policy.

Otherwise, where is the need? Laws have been invoked for years against religious sects that try to prevent children from receiving vital medical treatment. It is already illegal to raise children without some approved form of education. Child abuse and child neglect are crimes. What issues, then, should be actionable by children? A child's right to an abortion is one such issue, Hillary proclaims.

"Set aside the whole abortion issue," Barbara Olson wrote. "Set aside the fact, which Hillary herself presents, that courts will not hesitate to override the rights of parents to advance their perceptions of the health and safety of the child. The larger issue is that given the sort of lawsuit-crazy society in which we live—and I write as a lawyer myself—we know the answer is, yes, children *will* sue their parents over taking out the garbage, how late to stay out, and what clothes to wear and there *will* be lawyers who will argue that taking out the garbage is involuntary servitude."[47]

In her essay, Hillary reveals her view that the family and marriage are just artificial constructs—policies, really—that can be altered at will. "The basic rationale for depriving people of rights in a dependency relationship is that certain individuals are incapable or undeserving of the right to take care of themselves and consequently need social institutions specifically designed to safeguard their position.... Along with the family, past and present examples of such arrangements include marriage, slavery, and the Indian reservation system."

Here, Hillary took the family and its care of children, a relationship so basic to humanity that it preceded the last Ice Age, and dumped it into a category with Indian reservations and slavery.

Additionally, she discredits the concept of marriage. Both marriage and family are "dependency relationships" that require adjustment by her social engineers. Now, in *Living History*, she denies any radical intent behind her children's rights work or any radical consequences, despite the clear meaning of her early work. It is another lie, and a blatant one, but why should she not lie? The New Hillary, Senator Hillary Clinton, fears her past might damage her future political prospects—and when has lying ever imperiled her standing in the *Kultursmog*? Consider a final episode in her ideological biography; how, in a time of the highest national drama, the 1998 impeachment of her husband, she issued a set of lies that she stands by still, even though they are easily refuted.

She was no stranger to the issue of impeachment. In the 1970s, when young Hillary served as a staff member on the House Judiciary Impeachment Inquiry, she had been charged with surveying four centuries of common law in order to describe the intent of the constitutional provision for impeachment. Her report concluded that, "to limit impeachable conduct to criminal offenses would be incompatible with the evidence concerning the constitutional meaning of the phrase . . . and would frustrate the purpose that the framers intended for impeachment." As Maraniss points out, Hillary and her colleagues "found that in thirteen American impeachment cases, including ten of federal judges, less than one-third of the articles of impeachment explicitly charged the violation of a criminal statute."[48]

More than two decades later, as the wife of an impeached president, she took the opposite position, arguing that according to the Constitution only explicit felonies—apparently felonies graver than perjury—could trigger impeachment. Addressing House Democrats, she exploited the canard that the impeachment was only about sex.

She then admonished that to impeach a president on these (mostly) non-criminal grounds was a violation of the rule of law and of the Constitution. (In truth, President Clinton was impeachable both on criminal and non-criminal grounds—from perjury to obstruction of justice to abuse of power.) Hillary today praises her own 1974 work, saying that during the impeachment debacle of her husband, she often reread her old Watergate memos. She reports that she still agrees with her assessment.[49] Of course, her 1974 assessment is in stark contradiction to her more recent assessment, but Senator Clinton's reasonable calculation is that no one today is going to be so churlish as to mention it.

CHAPTER FIVE

The Coming Campaign

"When someone is beating you over the head with a hammer, don't sit there and take it. Take out a meat cleaver and cut off their hand."[1]

—*Bill Clinton, quoted by David Maraniss*

SENATOR CHARLES E. "CHUCK" SCHUMER entered the Lake Placid, New York, convention hall, his necktie swinging like a pendulum with his earnest stride. The son of a Brooklyn exterminator, Schumer became his high school's valedictorian, shined on the TV quiz show *It's Academic*, earned two degrees from Harvard, and became—at twenty-three years old—one of the youngest members of the New York State Assembly since Theodore Roosevelt. In 1980, at twenty-nine, he was elected to Congress. Schumer did not get to the Senate until 1998. Now he is the Empire State's senior senator, and here he was in Lake Placid, at one of those regional events that serve as national touchstones for ambitious Democrats.

No one noticed him arrive. When Schumer later stood at the podium, he denounced the shameless Republicans and their "crazy tax bill" with a passion that matched the fire and spittle of Michael Douglas's character in *The American President*. The ensuing applause was strong but brief. The audience was distracted. Someone else was in the hall.

Schumer, no fool, could not have been surprised at being upstaged. Hillary Rodham Clinton, his junior New York colleague, has been doing this to him for years—just by showing up. Schumer had been gamely hoping for the extra lift of a late arrival, pumping up the crowd and heightening the drama. But Hillary Clinton creates advantage by turning the rules upside down. She arrived *early* for the five-hour event, preceded as always by a palpable buzz, like the crest before a mighty ship. *Is she here yet? There's a big car outside—she's coming, I think she's coming. I see cameras—she must be here. She's here, she's here!*

And indeed, when she did walk in, it was within the hubbub of TV news cameras, klieg lights, and hefty security men. Hillary Clinton is a handsome woman, her search for the perfect hairstyle having finally been resolved with a neatly elegant businesswoman's coiffure. Her eyes are bright and observant. When she recognizes someone she likes, her face breaks into an expression of controlled glee, with wide-eyed, open-mouthed delight.

That night, just before the unveiling of her blockbuster memoir, the freshman senator was in Lake Placid to make small talk with Democratic county chairmen. Even in such commonplace settings, Hillary is the epicenter for the same relentless, unblinking coverage given to a United States president at a high-stakes Middle East peace conference.

Her opening remarks were prosaic. She did not hit her stride until she began to glow over the military exploits of that famous warrior-politician, George McGovern, as described in the late Stephen

Ambrose's book *The Wild Blue*. McGovern, she said, "was a TRUE military hero, and understood what the challenges of COMBAT actually WERE." On paper, even with the capital letters, this might read like merely a faint reproach to some unnamed non-veteran. In person, it had all the subtlety of raked knuckles across the face of George W. Bush, formerly of the Texas Air National Guard.

Now Hillary's blood was up. Her voice rose in modulated degrees toward outrage. She knows "what it takes to keep a great country great," and so she is astonished that this "administration is turning its back on the future." When President Bush came to office, she says, it was to undo the works of the previous administration. She did not like that, but she had to expect it.

But now look at what they've done.

"Two years ago we had a balanced budget," she says. "We had a surplus. We were paying down our debt. We were on the road to making our economy strong—far into the future." Of course, there had to be adjustments—that's part of the business cycle. "Yes, there are problems ahead for Social Security, Medicare and Medicaid. But under the previous administration," she says, "we had the resources in hand to deal with the problems everyone knew were on the horizon."

She is hectoring. Her pitch rises to the level of sarcasm when she imitates the despised Republicans: "What did *they* do? They came in and they said, 'We have a balanced budget, we have a surplus, in fact we have a projected surplus of $5.6 trillion. Well, we don't need that much of a surplus, so we can afford this extremely large tax cut, because we believe in supply-economics, and when we slash our revenues we get more revenues.' We've heard this before."

The sarcasm fairly drips. "You have to wonder: What is really happening here? How can people say with a straight face, 'Cut cut cut, and you will have more because supply-side economics will defy the laws of arithmetic?'

"What's going on here?" she asks again, then adds darkly: "There's another agenda at work."

That agenda, of course, is that of the Vast Right-Wing Conspiracy, unmasked a few years ago by Hillary herself on the *Today Show*. Hillary quotes her predecessor, the sainted Daniel Patrick Moynihan, to the effect that the Republicans are out to "starve the federal government, to prevent it from being able to do anything other than national defense." And so the Bush tax cut "is being funded by kicking 500,000 children out of after-school programs." She talks, too, about cuts in local funding for police, fire, and other local first providers in homeland defense. The implication is that the Bush administration is leaving America defenseless by refusing to send more grants to places like Buffalo and Utica.

Then the capper: "We fear for our country's future." The applause is sustained and deafening. It is a dark message, though political consultants will tell you that the American voter prefers optimism. It is a conspiratorial message, though political consultants will tell you that Americans eschew conspiracy theories. It is an argument centered on deficits, though the political graveyards are full of generations of Republicans—and more recently, of Democrats—who tried to get the American voters to care about deficits.

As usual, Hillary and her husband are their own best political consultants. This is no ordinary political speech—it is the early stump speech of a former president seeking to return to office. Hillary all but refers to the "buy one, get one free" administration, in which she was once famously considered to be a "co-president." When she talks of "bringing America back," she really means bringing back a Clinton presidency. She speaks as the once and future president.

When Senator John Kerry and Governor Howard Dean arrived in Lake Placid for a little presidential primary dustup, the conference has already been drained of energy and significance. The two front-runners for the Democratic nomination for the presidency made virtually no news. Instead, the headlines were dominated by a statement from Bill Clinton: that it might not be such a bad idea to strip term limits from the Constitution so that young presidents can have another crack at it.

The former president's statement was generally seen as a comic musing, not as a serious proposal. But it served its purpose. The tandem team of Bill and Hillary sucked up so much promotional "oxygen" that by the time Kerry and Dean showed up, Lake Placid might as well have been Mount Everest.

"The Candidate of Anger"

From her summer book tour to her startling presence as "master of ceremonies" at a fall showcase for the declared Democratic presidential candidates in Iowa, Hillary did all she could through 2003 to detract, distract, and denigrate her party's presidential hopefuls. It is likely no coincidence that Iowa governor Tom Vilsack—who, along with his wife, Christie, is a longtime friend of Hillary's—launched a lacerating attack on Howard Dean in November 2003, shortly after Hillary visited the state. The governor charged that Republicans could credibly attack Dean for not being "tough enough to pull the trigger" on Saddam Hussein. The emerging shape of Hillary's coming campaign for the presidency is also visible in the positions she is staking out and the political ground she is occupying. The most predictable aspect of her coming campaign is a renewal of her greatest strength in her 2000 Senate race—Hillary's appeal to Left-Behind America. This apt moniker is offered by Dr. John J. Pitney, Jr., a scholar of modern American politics and a professor of government at Claremont McKenna College, who observes: "Upstate New York and other parts of the Northeast are now what the South used to be, the left-behind part."

Grasping what Left-Behind America is all about is the key to understanding Hillary's appeal. The people of upstate New York were left behind when the economic center of gravity shifted to the Sun Belt, stilling the foundries and waterwheels of the industrial Empire State. Today, the small cities and towns of upstate New York are the kinds of places where a good day in business development consists of convincing a local couple to transform their charming Victorian into a B & B. The mainstay companies of the region—Kodak and Xerox—are struggling to modernize and compete, while the telecommunications meltdown has left Corning on the ropes.

In the 1990s, the region had high hopes that the era's general prosperity would spark an economic renaissance. It could have, and perhaps should have—cheap land, beautiful scenery and endless vistas, coupled with educated and hardworking people. Unfortunately, the 1990s brought almost nothing but an even more painfully acute sense of being left behind. While New York City boomed with immigrant energy and Silicon Alley entrepreneurialism, upstaters watched the high-tech Internet stock boom like a penniless child looking in a candy store window. Thus the early twenty-first century finds many upstate voters feeling that the game of life is rigged, that they have been cheated by downstate swindlers and Washington shenanigans, that the government owes them some payback. These are the downsized, the fed up.

In short, these are Hillary's people. Disposition is important in politics, perhaps more important than intellect. Hillary's disposition is dark, sour, conspiratorial. She always has a ready pitch for the pessimists, especially those who feel large forces are manipulating them. "She became the candidate of anger," says Bill Dal Col, a veteran Kemp and Forbes strategist who mounted a heroic effort to revive Congressman Rick Lazio's moribund Senate campaign against Hillary in 2000. While Republicans tend to see the American people as comfortably suburban, Hillary has dug deeper, discovering rich veins of resentment in discarded parts of Middle America.

The Republicans learned this after their expensive upstate ad blitz in 2000 proved futile. Hillary understood that what upstate's Left Behind wanted was connection, a sense that somebody cared about them. She established a connection by launching a superbly organized grassroots campaign. There is, to be sure, a kind of Potemkin village aspect to her "listening tours," a long, dreary public service chore meant to spotlight her earnestness and caring. The listening tour was a product Hillary initially devised as first lady of Arkansas, in a campaign to consolidate the governor's power over the schools. She began her campaign by visiting every one of Arkansas's seventy-five counties, sitting in committee meetings that lasted as long as nine hours.[2] (Once a politician finds something that works, it never drops out of the repertoire.) As a senator, Hillary has allowed her connection to the farthest reaches of upstate to languish. In pursuing the Senate, however, Hillary toured all of New York state's sixty-two counties in her

Ford conversion van, dubbed the HRC Speedwagon. She canvassed the diners and sampled the local pies, making admiring comments about the cherry filling. She understood that for people traumatized by being left behind, just dropping by and sampling the pie can be an act of solidarity.[3]

In her memoir, Hillary made an observation about Left-Behind America that could be taken as a blueprint for her coming campaign. She wrote, "Parts of upstate New York reminded me of neighboring Pennsylvania, where my father had roots. And many of rural New York's problems were similar to those that had plagued Arkansas: hard-pressed farmers, disappearing manufacturing jobs and young people leaving for better opportunities."[4]

Hillary is nothing if not an astute sentinel of political change. With manufacturing jobs disappearing and factories closing, there are many places in America that resemble her description of upstate New York. While Republicans tend to view middle-class America as McLean, Virginia; North Dallas, Texas; or Orange County, California, Hillary and her people have a keen appreciation that the "red" part of the map that voted for George W. Bush is pocketed with left-behind communities that could easily go "blue," from the textile towns in North Carolina to laid-off tech and telecom workers in Houston and Austin to the downsized white-collar workers who once worked at AT&T in New Jersey or at Boeing in Seattle. In better times, many of these people would vote Republican, but they're up for grabs now.

Hard times will not transform these Americans into Maoists. It will make them, however, receptive to the candidate of the listening tour, who responds to their complaints, nurses their resentments, and exploits their fears. This is why Hillary's first dramatic move on the Senate floor was to push the extension of unemployment benefits. She knows who her people are. She also knows how to act like she is still one of them.

Saul Alinsky preached that the activist should return to his middle-class roots. Alinsky wrote, "His middle-class identity, his familiarity with the values and problems, are invaluable for organization of his 'own people.' He has the background to go back, examine, and try to understand the middle-class way. . . . He will know that a 'square' is no longer to be dismissed as such—instead, his own approach must be 'square' enough to get the action started."[5]

One should especially cultivate the lower middle class, Alinsky counseled. On this subject, he writes as if he were a voyaging anthropologist covertly observing the habits of a curious people: "Their pleasures are simple: gardening a tiny back yard behind a small house, bungalow, or ticky-tacky, in a monotonous subdivision on the fringe of the suburbs; going on a Sunday drive out to the country, having a once-a-week dinner at some place like a Howard Johnson's. Many of the so-called hard hats, police, fire, sanitation workers, schoolteachers, and much of civil service, mechanics, electricians, janitors, and semi-skilled workers are in this class."[6] Hillary's floor speeches are often a paean to these very job categories.

Once the activist reacclimates to a milieu, at once familiar and exotic, the time comes to exploit the native's naïve lack of political consciousness. "So you return to the suburban scene of your middle class, with its variety of organizations from PTAs to League of Women Voters, consumer groups, churches, and clubs," Alinksy directs. "The job is to search out the leaders in these various activities, identify their major issues, find areas of common agreement, and excite their imagination with tactics that can introduce drama and adventure into the tedium of middle-class life."[7]

Hillary's life—lived out in a backdrop of politics and travel—is a steady adventure. Posting yard signs and walking precincts, for her, is just one small way to bring a little of her adventure into one's Left-Behind life. Knowing this, Hillary strives to heighten the adventure for all her followers by addressing economic and cultural issues in terms that are positively Manichean. Hillary calls these "kitchen table" issues, but the inflammatory rhetoric turns them into a life-and-death *Kulturkampf* against the pure evils of Republicanism.

Thus, tax cuts are not just a matter of sound economics. "Every decision we make about taxes is a decision about our values," she says. As with spending money on rebuilding Iraq, the issue of tax cuts is endlessly elastic. It can be blamed for anything and everything. It is responsible for the closure of firehouses. It is responsible for the laying off of police officers, "the very soldiers we need to help us fight that war and protect our homeland." It is responsible for state budget deficits. It is responsible for the rising requests for food stamps and housing assistance in Steuben County, New York.[8]

When Hillary attacks Bush, she speaks as "the daughter of a small businessman who did not believe in living outside our means and who even paid cash for the house we lived in." She denounces the president's tax cuts, which spend "trillions we don't have, and may never have."[9] Hillary's pose as the daughter of a spendthrift lets her have it both ways—while she denounces Bush for cutting taxes, she can also denounce him for letting spending get out of control. Never mind that much of it is driven by the opening investment in homeland defense. Hillary, taught by Hugh Rodham to conserve toothpaste, would never let things get so badly out of control.

At first, it is difficult to perceive the future in her argument, especially if she wants to set herself up for 2008. The economy in 2004 is clearly gearing up for growth. Bush will surely get the domestic side of the budget under better control, while no one can dispute the need for a higher level of spending on defense. Hillary is not oblivious to the main chance. She is looking ahead to that pregnant moment near the end of the first decade of the twenty-first century, when the nation is faced with the realization that our shrinking ratio of workers to retirees can no longer support Social Security and Medicare.

The Bush tax cut, of course, has nothing to do with constraints in Social Security and Medicare—demographics tells us that those constraints are coming whether we cut taxes, raise taxes, or replace the dollar with the euro. But Hillary is anticipating the politics of 2008, when the first baby boomers enter retirement and the mounting pressure of entitlement spending begins wringing out every budget item save defense. Hillary often approvingly quotes her predecessor Daniel Patrick Moynihan to the effect that starving government is what Republicans want to do. Moynihan was right—Republicans do want that (indeed, they admit it publicly). Hillary understands that the elementary school teacher, fireman, and dairy farmer will not like the sound of that. She is preparing for these politics of budgetary constraints, setting up Republicans and their fiscal policies to take the fall for the inevitable constraints of entitlement programs collapsing under their own demographic weight.

Most politicians fear the political chaos that the impending Social Security and Medicare crash will create. Hillary knows that chaos clears a path for radical changes, like electing the first woman president with a leftist background. That is why she is working so hard now to set up Republicans to take the fall.

"[W]e're sailing on a sea with a big rogue wave headed our way," Hillary said in a speech to the American Society of Newspaper

Editors. "That wave is called the 'retirement of the baby boomers.' You could call it 'invasion of the surplus snatcher.' And do you know when that wave hits? It hits a year after this ten-year surplus projection ends. How convenient for those who argue for the big tax cut! They don't have to account for what's facing our Social Security and Medicare systems. And they don't take into account what we need to do now to shore up and reform those important safeguards for older Americans."[10]

If she runs in 2008, Hillary will be the candidate of blame. While going on the economic offense, however, Hillary will have to play defense on social issues. This is because the issues are blurring, and she must struggle to adapt.

One part of this changing landscape is a slightly different Republican Party. On the Left Coast, Governor Schwarzenegger is a tax-cutting, budget-cutting reader of Milton Friedman, who is pro-choice but anti–partial-birth abortion and is comfortable with gays and gay domestic partnerships, though a supporter of the idea that marriage is solely between a man and a woman. "If Arnold becomes governor, the entire dynamic changes," one producer said shortly before the 2003 California election. "He automatically becomes the presumptive liaison between Bush and the entertainment industry. He will take with him a fair number of middle-of-the-road Democrats, who will be in with Bush. This will drive the left crazy." Meanwhile, in the White House, President Bush has moved the Republican Party toward a pragmatic approach on abortion; he signed the partial-birth abortion ban into law but conceded that America is not ready for a total ban on abortions. President Bush has made it possible to be both pro-life and pragmatic.

This is happening because President Bush—who is adamantly pro-life and deeply worried about the implications of cloning and other research on embryos—knows that the best way to fight abortion is to win hearts and minds, and he knows that they're being won. This is the second complicating factor for Hillary and her core of feminist supporters. What years of political debates could not achieve, the sonogram has. Millions of American women who were once adamantly pro-choice soften and change their views once they get a sonogram and see the unmistakable features of a living, squirming baby inside them.

This is what the Center for the Advancement of Women, headed by longtime abortion-rights advocate Faye Wattleton, learned when it conducted an in-depth survey. The Center found that a majority of American women met some definitions of the pro-life position. In fact, 51 percent believe that the government should prohibit abortion, or limit it to extreme cases such as rape, incest, or life-threatening complications. This was a dramatic increase in pro-life sentiment from 2001, when 45 percent of women were opposed to abortion. The percentage of women who support making abortion generally available declined from 34 percent to 30 percent.[11]

Such an environment poses risks for Hillary. Once, it was the pro-life side that had to endure constant portrayals as "extremist." Now it is the turn of the pro-choice side to wear that mantle, with Hillary, Chuck Schumer, and a minority of thirty-four senators standing pat in voting against a ban on partial-birth abortions (a procedure Moynihan once deemed "infanticide"). Sixty-four members of the Senate, including Democratic minority leader Tom Daschle and other liberal stalwarts like Joseph Biden and Ernest Hollings, found the practice repugnant enough to vote against it. As the issue drags on in the courts, it is Hillary who faces the danger of being seen as extreme.

Here again, Hillary remains an acute sentinel of political change. She has come up with a new position on abortion, one that she casts in Cold War terms that are almost Reaganesque. Hillary sets up this rationale in *Living History*, writing of admonitions on abortion from Mother Teresa that "were always loving and heartfelt." Then Hillary spells out why she cannot accept spiritual direction even from the beatified. "I had the greatest respect for her opposition to abortion, but I believe that it is dangerous to give any state the power to enforce criminal penalties against women and doctors," Hillary writes. "I consider that a slippery slope to state control of reproduction, and I'd witnessed the consequences of such control in China and Communist Romania."[12] So, you see, Hillary's concern is really about communism and an overweening state. This line may strike some as preposterous. But it is sure to have a certain electoral appeal. The vulnerability in Hillary's position emerges when one rereads her statement and spots the key role played by the phrase "any state." When democratically elected representatives pass reasonable restrictions on abortion in American states—requiring parental notification for teenagers, or restricting late-term abortions—is that really tantamount to letting the Red Army control the wombs of American women? For that matter, when *Roe v. Wade* struck down the abortion laws of all fifty states, enacted by the democratically elected representatives of the people, and replaced them with a Supreme Court ukase based on a newly discovered "penumbra" in the Constitution, was that a triumph of democracy? For Republicans, campaigning against overweening courts—and the liberals who support them—in favor of "letting the people decide" is a winning issue.

Hillary will struggle in many other ways to sound as if she is running to the right, just as Bill did when he attacked rapper Sister Souljah for rhapsodizing about homicide. At the point that Hillary believes herself to have the reins of the nomination securely in her hands, the Rev.

Al Sharpton could play a convenient role as a Souljah-like rhetorical foil—even as she continues to speak at AME churches and pushes for federal legislation to eliminate racial profiling by the police. The same woman who twice invited Dick Morris to save Bill's career has, by now, internalized the lessons of Morris. She will know how to triangulate.

For that reason, she cannot be surprised, or displeased, by press reports that she rankled the anti-war left with her nuanced support of President Bush's war against Iraq, or that she upset her old friends from the Children's Defense Fund by supporting proposals to stiffen the work requirement for welfare recipients. At the same time, she cannot go too far from her base. Pollsters in both political parties are finding that the independent swing vote has shrunk a bit. There is a growing recognition that party-line voters are more partisan than ever before. Getting out the base vote is now the surest way of increasing turnout.

If Hillary is to win, she will need to reach to the center while keeping the base enthusiastic and energized. This will not be a challenge. Any estrangement from the left is unlikely to be permanent—not for the chairman of the Senate Steering Committee, the point person for protest campaigns against Bush judicial nominees. Like Ronald Reagan, Hillary enjoys a comfort level with her party's base that is secure enough to let her explore the center. Thus she is free to exchange pleasantries with the centrist Democratic Leadership Council and its leader, Al From. Her husband did the same in his long pre-presidential phase. Hillary-as-moderate is yet another exercise in rebranding, moving forward with all the spontaneity of a North Korean placard-card pageant.

She is not likely to repeat Al Gore's blunder of running on class warfare. She will most likely stick with centrist pollster Mark Penn rather than the more liberal Stan Greenberg. Looking at the map, Hillary will be able to count on the support of Tom and Christie Vilsack. Personal testimonials from Iowa's first couple will count for a lot in the coffee klatch intimacy of the caucus.

The Northeast and the West Coast—though the Democrats will now have to fight to keep California—will ultimately go to Hillary. In the balance, the contest will come down to Michigan, Pennsylvania, and a host of small swing states, from Missouri to New Mexico. Florida, as before, will be on a razor's edge. Hillary attracts more women voters than even her husband. She beat Lazio among upstate New York women by a margin of 55 percent to 43 percent. Her greatest strength will be her connection with American women and an ability to grasp and communicate her concern for issues about which the average male Republican is oblivious, beginning with the time-stressed life of the American family. In *Living History*, she writes about listening to a working single mother in New York City tell how every minute of her day is precariously scheduled from dawn to dusk, from ironing while her nine-year-old eats breakfast to working as an executive secretary to coming home at the exact moment the after-school program ends. This is not a federal issue. But then, Hillary does not have to do anything to get this woman's vote except listen to her.[13]

Hillary is also alert to the fact that the "gender gap" works both ways. Democrats may have an advantage in attracting the votes of women, but they have often paid for this by losing the votes of men, especially working men.

Hillary is furiously adapting and spinning her positions on national defense issues, the defense of the homeland, and U.S. foreign policy to win the votes of men. Throughout her years as co-president, Hillary's main interest in foreign policy was to shift the State Department and international lending agencies to support the education of girls, the empowerment of women, and the internationalization of the feminist agenda. After September 11, 2001, Hillary is wide awake to the need to be less a feminist icon and children's rights advocate, and more of a card-carrying member of the Truman wing of the Democratic Party.

Following in the footsteps of Cold Warriors like the late Henry "Scoop" Jackson does not come naturally to Hillary. She must to do her homework to be convincing. A close observer of the Armed Services Committee privately detailed Hillary's unusual interest in the painstaking process of "markup," the fine-tuning and fleshing out of the inner workings of a bill, in this case the Defense Authorization Bill. These are tedious affairs usually left to the professional staff of the relevant committees. Hillary attended almost every minute of markup over three days.

"Every single other senator comes and goes, except for one person, who takes notes, bright-eyed over every boring piece," this observer said. From morning until late at night, Hillary absorbed the construction of the bill, from the provision of health benefits to service families to the bill's Classified Annex of "black" budget items.

Part of her intention, of course, is to burnish her national security credentials, to be able to talk military acronyms with the best of them. But there is more. "The way anti-military Democrats have done things and stayed viable is by supporting military housing, and military and veterans' welfare," the observer said. "That way, they can get the endorsement of veterans' organizations without actually having to support weapons systems."

When it comes to weapons, however, Hillary is no longer a doctrinaire liberal. She recognizes that the days are over for the "nuclear freeze," as well as the strident opposition to missile defense. She also knows, as not one of her constituents in New York City can forget, the truth in JFK's observation that "domestic policy can only defeat us; foreign policy can kill us." This gives her the impetus to reach toward the center. She broke with the left to give her highly nuanced and conditional support in authorizing President Bush to go to war with Iraq. In so doing, she broke with her own husband, who took a much more dovish position. "The break with Bill actually helps her," says a reporter who covers the Clintons. "She shows she's independent of him. She comes off more center-right, with a wider base."

When Hillary went to Baghdad in November 2003 to have dinner with the troops, she soon found herself upstaged by President Bush, who had slipped into the war zone in secrecy. Throughout the years of the Clinton presidency, the Clintons had artfully used the trappings of the office to upstage their opponents. Now it was Hillary's turn to be diminished by the man with the big blue airplane.

Once before the troops, Hillary applauded them while denouncing the approach of the Bush administration. Her speech did not win her many plaudits (indeed, so few U.S. military personnel volunteered to meet with her that military leaders in Baghdad had to order enlisted personnel and junior officers to spend time with her.)

"Her husband didn't get it and she obviously hasn't learned," an American staffer in Baghdad told the *American Spectator*'s Prowler. "These men and women over here are America. They are the policy. For her to say what she said was just misguided." Of course, Hillary knew better. The troops were not her intended audience. They were a serviceable backdrop for a choice bit of agitprop, words to energize the left, and a photo-op with Americans in uniform to calm middle America.[14] One suspects that the Clintons conspire to create such a contrast. The reality remains that the contrast works for the half of the partnership of Clinton & Clinton that is still eligible for national office. She is very open about her relationship with her husband—at least the political side of it. When asked by a German magazine why she was not running for president, Hillary replied, "Well, perhaps I'll do it next time around." Later, she spoke of her relationship with Bill Clinton. "It is actually a kind of job rotation. First, Bill focused on his career, now it's my turn. Bill supports me and gives me tips, he's my best adviser, as I tried to be for him when he was fulfilling political office."[15]

The political dynamic changes on homeland defense. Here, women are more responsive to this concern than men. Any New York politician would need a high profile on this issue. Hillary's primary policy is to position herself as the nation's purveyor of blame after the next terrorist attack.

"GOP used to mean Grand Old Party. But more and more it's standing for 'Gloss Over Problems,'" she told the Democratic Leadership Council in 2002.

She segues into her policy, arguing that the Bush administration cannot be serious about homeland defense until it has fortified every small city and town in America.

"Our vigilance has faded at the top, in the corridors of power in Washington, D.C., where the strategy and resources to protect our nation are supposed to originate," she said in an address at John Jay College, "where leaders are supposed to lead. Our constitutional imperative, to 'provide for the common defense,' has not been fully realized. As a result, our people remain vulnerable, nearly as vulnerable as they were before 8:46 a.m. on September 11. And here in New York, that complacency doesn't just threaten our security, it tears at our hearts."

This is Hillary's trademark Manichean approach: question an opponent's motives. The dubious motive she attributes to the Bush administration is personal greed; presumably the Bushies enrich themselves and their corporate co-conspirators by shoveling home-land security dollars to friendly corporations. Once again, Hillary says, the problem is that homeland security dollars are not "getting to most of our cities and towns." The reason is the perfidious Bush tax cut. "Will ending the dividend tax make air travel safer? Will it secure our nuclear power plants? Will it keep a dirty bomb out of New York harbor?"[16]

As silly as her rhetoric might strike some today, it is important to always keep in mind that Hillary is not speaking to the present. She is positioning herself for the future so that on the day after our next major terror attack she can say "I told you so" and demand "an expla-nation."

Another aspect of Hillary's new centrism is her public concern for the survival of Israel. Madame Hillary, during her days as first lady of Arkansas, had chaired a leftist organization, the New World Founda-tion, which funneled grants to PLO front groups. As first lady of the United States, she had called for a Palestinian state, in defiance of offi-cial American policy. And of course, as first lady of the United States, Hillary had been widely criticized for her public display of affection to Suha Arafat following Mrs. Arafat's diatribe against the Jewish state. Now the woman who was widely believed to have been a prime mover behind the Oslo Peace Accords defends Israel as it suffers the conse-quences of Oslo. She publicly expresses doubt about Arafat's sincerity as a negotiator for peace. This is partly because Arafat's duplicity is so obvious, and partly because the United States has more Jewish voters than Israel. (In *Living History*, Hillary strains to show us pictures and tell us about her grandmother's Jewish husband.)[17]

Hillary knows that despite her recent modifications, she may well be playing defense on questions concerning the Middle East. President

Truman recognized the Jewish state. President Nixon defended it. But no president has been closer to the concerns and interests of Israel than George W. Bush.

Another point of vulnerability for Hillary in post–September 11 America is Bill's explicit admission that he rejected an offer from Sudan in 1996 to arrest and extradite Osama bin Laden. This was long after bin Laden had been tied to the first attack on the World Trade Center in 1993. Richard Miniter, in an impressively researched book, *Losing bin Laden*, weaves an account based on extensive interviews with high-ranking intelligence and foreign policy officials to show how Clinton labored to keep terrorism on the back burner. Clinton wanted terror to be treated as a criminal matter, not a security matter, and thus keep it off the political radar screen. When the World Trade Center was bombed in 1993, Miniter reports, the decision by the Clinton administration to treat this act of terror as a criminal matter meant that the FBI could not share information with the Central Intelligence Agency without also sharing it with the accused terrorists. Clinton's response to the truck bombing of American service personnel in Saudi Arabia and to the bombings of the East African embassies was minimal. Following the attack on the USS *Cole* that left seventeen sailors dead, the forty-second president did nothing, according to Miniter. In Miniter's account, after the *Cole* incident Secretary of State Madeleine Albright remonstrated against a military response, lest it derail the Middle East peace process—then the prime objective of a president yearning for a Nobel Peace Prize as an antidote to impeachment.

The Clinton people now protest that the Sudan offer might not have been sincere. But the evidence is that the offer was genuine. Before bin Laden, Carlos the Jackal was the world's most wanted terrorist. When asked to give him up, Sudan produced him. Why not Osama?

In responding to this question, Hillary showed that her tendency to speak as the once and future president could imperil her coming campaign. Hillary looked pretty bad when she was surprised by a question from Newsmax's Carl Limbacher on a talk radio show. Asked about her husband's rejection of the Sudan offer, Hillary responded, "But remember, when *we* were looking to try to deal with bin Laden, there wasn't any, at that point, any absolute linkage, as there later became, with both the bombings in Africa and the USS *Cole*. And it was also the fact that I think it's hard for *us* now to remember, that the United States, at that point in time, as well as our allies, had a very different mindset about the best way to deal with these potential problems around the world. *We* didn't have the support of the country's intelligence agencies that we were able to obtain after 9/11." (Emphasis added.)[18]

Put aside the subtle shifting of blame to the CIA. Hillary looks preposterous when she speaks of herself as a former president. Nonetheless her memoirs are full of such reckless language. In one passage, she speaks of taking political advantage of then–Speaker of the House Newt Gingrich. She writes, "Newt Gingrich handed *me* the perfect opportunity." (Emphasis added.)[19] She writes not of a perfect opportunity for her husband, the president, or for the "administration," but *me. The co-president.* By inserting herself into her husband's presidency she appears appallingly vain, and she risks carrying with her the baggage of all the decisions of the Clinton years.

Hillary's handlers have to be worried about her tendency to get too far out front, whereupon she becomes her own worst enemy. Every politician enjoys cycles of rising and declining popularity. Hillary's peaks and troughs are colossal. As popular as she became after the publication of *Living History*, it is important to remember that in

1996—ravaged by the health care debacle and Whitewater—Hillary became the only first lady in three decades of polling to have a majority unfavorable rating, 51 percent. In that year, a *USA Today/* CNN/Gallup poll found that 52 percent of the America people believed she was a liar; and an astonishing 68 percent say she probably did something illegal or unethical. In the aftermath of her Senate election, with the furor over auctioned pardons and stolen furniture, Hillary once again approached rock bottom. She could land there again.

There are many dangers in her path. Hillary breaks with her Senate colleague Chuck Schumer by refusing to release her tax returns. What is she hiding? She might continue to shriek, as she occasionally does in her speeches to the party faithful, slipping into hyperbole about Bush that makes her sound ridiculous to most of America. Will she be caught again rolling her eyes during a presidential address? In a presidential race, shadowy figures like Harold Ickes and Susan Thomases will become known to the American people, and they will not appear pretty under the klieg lights. The public may catch a glimpse of how hard Hillary can be on her staff (she was, according to one New York politico, exceptionally tough on her media lieutenant, Howard Wolfson).[20] Will the public catch a glimpse of what one Rose Law Firm associate once described to the *New Yorker*: "It's not so much that she screams—it's more the tone in her voice, the body language, the facial expressions. It's 'The Wrath of Khan.'"?[21]

Above all, will she succumb to the same relentless negativism that seems to be the only message of the other Democrats who want to be president? "Democrats used to say, we have nothing to fear but fear itself," a Bush administration aide says. "Now they say, 'fear is our most important product.'"[22]

Another potential vulnerability is what to do with Bill. "Two-for-one worked when it was Hillary being sold as the first spouse," a national political correspondent says. "She was a smart, professional woman, not your traditional first lady. That was the bargain deal, and a plurality of the American people accepted it or overlooked it. This time, the other half of that bargain is going to be a former president. How are they going to sell it? How's she gonna deal with him? There's no reason to believe she'd be happy about having her presidency as Bill Clinton's third term."

Just as Bill overshadows the current field of Democratic presidential aspirants, might he also be unable to restrain himself from jumping into the middle of his wife's campaign? And then there is the question of whether the public will want to bring Bill Clinton's sexual lifestyle back into the White House. For these reasons, Hillary might want to engineer an amicable divorce from Bill. After all, it would take very little work to find fresh grounds for such a divorce (indeed, one might wonder if squibs in the New York press reporting Hillary's pique over Bill's paramours are setting the groundwork for such a move). Bill is a private detective's dream. How could he not go along? Hillary could tell the nation that she still loves Bill, always will, that they had a great marriage, it had its ups and downs, produced a wonderful child, now it is time to move on, etc. If the divorce is finalized before her 2006 reelection bid to the Senate, it could spark a whole new "you go, girl" wave of enthusiasm among American women. Following Hillary's emancipation would be the blaze of publicity that would attend the spectacle of Hillary dating eligible and appropriately emasculated men. "You go, girl" could put her into the White House.

Or, she might opt to stick with Bill, with all the attendant risks he entails. Either way, Hillary will be able to count on William Jefferson

Clinton to serve as de facto campaign adviser and chief fund-raiser. Their marriage might expire, but it is difficult to imagine the political team known in Arkansas as "Billary" being separated by divorce or, indeed, anything short of death.

Candidate When?

Of the forty-three Americans who have been elected president, fifteen were former senators, including Andrew Jackson and Harry Truman. Only two presidents, Warren G. Harding and John F. Kennedy, moved directly from the Senate chambers to the Oval Office. For Hillary to be the third senator—and the first woman—would be a hat trick. But then, what is the career of both Clintons if not a succession of hat tricks?

The question of the moment is: "When?" Many veteran Hillary-watchers are adamant that she will not jump in the 2004 race. "She's too smart to contest anyone in a primary," Philip Kawior predicts. "She's going to wait for the Democrats' implosion." New York's Bill Dal Col agrees. "I don't think she sees herself as having spent enough time in the vineyard to make wine."

Though the numbers have tightened, it is likely that Hillary will not forget that a Quinnipiac poll showed President Bush beating her 52 percent to 41 percent in a hypothetical match-up. Nor is she likely to forget the Marist poll in 2003 that 69 percent of New Yorkers polled want her to stay in the Senate and forego a 2004 presidential bid. "She'll play with it, run with it, dance with it—but Hillary is far too smart to get sucked into the vortex," Dal Col predicted in 2003.

Who might oppose Hillary if she goes in 2008? The Republican Party will have a strong bench: Senate majority leader Bill Frist, the nation's avuncular family doctor; George Allen, the Virginia senator who exudes a touch of the old Reagan magic; Colorado governor Bill Allen, the most successful and respected governor in America; and there are others. There are some wild cards, one of them being the president's brother. Even those close to the Bushes wonder if "Bush fatigue" would rule out Florida governor Jeb Bush. "It even bothers me a little, and I like Jeb," said an aide to the elder Bush. "You would have to contend with the Bush dynasty thing. It's different when you have the father passing it down to the sons, the princes so to speak. With the Clintons, the presidency would not be passed *down* from Bill to Hillary. It would be passed *across*."

Then again, Jeb might be viable if he ends his governorship in Florida on a good note, and his brother ends his presidency with a high approval rating. Jeb speaks Spanish, and even more astonishing for a member of the Bush family, he speaks English as well.

Another wild card, of course, is Rudy Giuliani. Giuliani has the stature to challenge Hillary's toughness without coming across like a bully, and he can match her in celebrity. But his social liberalism could seriously depress the turnout of religious conservatives who are crucial to Republican victory in the South and the swing states. If Giuliani were to take on Hillary, he would have to modify his position or would be better placed to challenge her for the Senate in 2006.

Any of these Republicans could be her opponent. One thing Hillary can count on: she won't have to contend with a Republican woman at the top of the ticket.

"Elizabeth Dole, no one wants to see that again," says a national political correspondent. "Other than that, Republicans have tried to elevate women. There were high hopes for Susan Molinari. That went nowhere. Republicans had high hopes for Kay Bailey Hutchinson, but she's too old and may run for governor." But what about a woman on the ticket as vice president?

Consider Dr. Condoleezza Rice. If Dr. Rice becomes Secretary of State in a second Bush term—which seems likely at this writing—she will be on any prospective nominee's short list as vice president. Even in 2008, a ticket with a young African-American woman will be an electrifying event, one that would drain much of the novelty from Hillary's campaign.

We cannot know what America will be like in 2008. It is likely, however, that the election of 2008 will be a contest of giants. In running that gauntlet, Hillary will be facing the last obstacle between herself and the White House. She is not likely to forget the advice of Saul Alinsky: "The enemy properly goaded and guided in his reaction will be your major strength."[23] Any Republican who faces her will certainly be "properly goaded." Of that we can be certain.

CHAPTER SIX

Fatal Attraction

"Democrats exulted when Bill Clinton seemed to be paying no price for his personal shortcomings in the 1992 and 1996 elections, and in the impeachment controversy. But nothing in politics is free; there is only some question about when you pay the price. Democrats may end up paying the price for Gennifer Flowers and Monica Lewinsky, Whitewater and Travelgate, in 2008."[1]

—*Michael Barone*

SINCE THE CLINTONS' DEPARTURE FROM the White House, a large number of Democratic professionals have come down with what the clinically minded call schizophrenia. At least, these Dems are schizo about the Clintons. In early 2000, the Democrats' schizophrenia intensified as the media howled about the Clintons' brazen pardons and the White House property that had found its way into their moving vans.

Party strategists and lobbyists were delighted with the Clintons' many tactical victories over the hapless Republicans, but were also aware of a prickly little fact. Across America, the happy rank-and-file Democrats had savored each Clinton victory: the humbling of Newt Gingrich, the diabolizing of Ken Starr, the spectacle of their impeached president overcoming more allegations than Richard

Nixon and Spiro Agnew. Yet party strategists and lobbyists recognized that each Clinton victory came at the end of many costly battles, some of which never should have been fought. Almost all were battles that did nothing to strengthen or extend Democratic influence nationally. In fact, the battles damaged the party's reputation, certainly with independent voters and with voters who worried about ethics in public life. Impeachment over a tart boasting of her thong underwear? An eight-year investigation of real estate chicanery that not even the Harding administration would have been a party to? What kind of victories are these?

Yes, the Democratic professionals relished seeing the Clintons best the Republicans, but they also recognize that for the national Democratic Party there have been long-term strategic costs concomitant with the Clintons' endless episodes of the Perils of Pauline. Many party professionals and many principled liberals fully realize that as long as the Democratic Party is willing to put its reputation on the line for the Clintons, it will be in danger of serving only as a transport for the Clintons' personal ambitions.

And one thing more—the core of the Democratic party in the aftermath of the calamitous Clinton presidency is in danger of becoming a core whose hot button issues are "conspiracies on the right," "the politics of personal destruction," and other such esotery. If that becomes the Democratic platform, the party will become a ghost ship to oblivion.

This is the secret concern of many party professionals and traditional liberals. Their distrust and fear of the Clintons explains much of the impetus behind the Dean Machine. Assuming that Dean does not become president—and therefore lacks the power to pry the Democratic Party from the grasp of the Clintons—we are left to ask:

What is happening to the party of Jefferson and Jackson, the party that led America through two world wars?

"Could someone please tell these people to shut up?" asked Susan Estrich, one of the most ardent liberal voices on the West Coast. "The Democrats might have a chance of electing a new president if they could get the last one, and his defenders, to clear the stage. It doesn't matter if they're right or wrong. They should be history."[2]

In the twenty-first century, the symbiotic relationship between the Clintons and their party is growing, but Bill and Hillary are increasingly beginning to look like millstones on a party that should be preparing to sprint. Nonetheless, the Clintons cannot be shaken. Their servitors are stationed throughout the party and its strongholds in the *Kultursmog.*

Hillary and Bill dominate others with the inexhaustible energy of lifelong egotists. They are forever on the march and on the make. At times, it almost seems the Clintons are at play with the party's other leading figures. Throughout the spring and summer of 2003, as the Democratic presidential candidates launched their campaigns and earnestly elbowed each other out of the limelight, the Clintons effortlessly hogged the show whenever they wished. Hillary had her grand book tour and occasional Solomonic pronouncements. Bill had such high jinks as his very public musings on whether the constitutional amendment barring two-term presidents should endure; his delightful counseling of California's doomed governor, Gray Davis; and his unexpected words of understanding for President George W. Bush (who was at the time being called a *liar* for sixteen incautious words in his State of the Union address).

Yet if Bill's efforts appeared playful and capricious, Senator Clinton was all business. Taken together, the Clintons' easy grasp of the limelight made the lackluster Democratic presidential candidates appear all the more feckless. Every time Dr. Howard Dean or Senator John Kerry aroused a slight rustling on the hustings, a Clinton eruption distracted the media's attention. By late summer 2003, the stage was set for Hillary to emerge as the frontrunner for the next political cycle, during which she could practice her splendid aloofness while the declared candidates floundered.

Madame Hillary has always been an opportunist. Senator Hillary is a *suave* opportunist. That is a significant evolution in Hillary Rodham Clinton's style. As her plain-speaking Tammany Hall predecessor, Boss George Washington Plunkitt, was wont to say generations ago, so too New York's junior senator can say today, "I seen my opportunities and I took 'em."

Hillary's syntax might be more polished than the Boss's, but he was more candid. She's looking for her opportunity, and when she takes it, Hillary will be a polarizing force, electrifying the Clinton hardcore and alienating an equal proportion of the electorate. Will she prove to be the Democrats' heroine or its curse?

"Name a speaker in the Democratic Party today who has the voice, the music, that Democrats want to hear?" asks Republican Philip Kawior. "Only Hillary—the others offer no pizzazz, no hope. There is no one else who serves as the vessel that you want to put your and your family's aspirations into. They're not there."

The Power of Myth

Millions of Democrats' unshakable fealty to the Clintons cannot be understood without grasping how the power of myth has shaped and energized the modern Democratic Party. Of the two major parties, the Democratic Party is the mythopoeic party. The Republican

Party is the party of commerce and of the dull sober virtues of commerce in Middle America. Such values do not encourage political drama. They encourage economic growth or law and order, but not New Deals, New Frontiers, or Bill Clinton's Bridge to the Twenty-first Century, whatever that might be.

The Democrats' aptitude for myth has created the mythical American presidency, or at least the mythical American presidency of the twentieth century. This presidency strides through the *Kultursmog*, the politically polluted *kultur* conferred on America by its liberal elites. There in the *Kultursmog* there is no heroism associated with the golfer, Ike, or the actor, Reagan. They are mediocrities in the *Kultursmog*'s version of American history. But Woodrow Wilson! FDR! JFK! and, in a baggy pants, hang-dog way, Bill Clinton—all embody the myths that make an American president great and *very* dramatic—at least as presented to us in the *Kultursmog*.

Not surprisingly, all the mythical American presidents of the twentieth century were Democrats, save the first, Theodore Roosevelt. Yet, he was a progressive, and progressives in the early twentieth century were today's liberals' intellectual and spiritual antecedents. From TR to Woodrow Wilson, thence to Franklin Roosevelt and then John F. Kennedy, the liberal mythmakers (mostly Democrats such as professor James McGregor Burns and the tireless professor Arthur Schlesinger, Jr., and more recently professor Sean Wilentz of Princeton) kept piling on the myths. None has ever been discarded.

Up there in the *Kultursmog,* the mythical American president is compassionate and a champion of the underdog. He is intellectual with a taste for poetry and fine food. He laughs heartily and is handsome. He is very tough but very kindly. He is athletic, adventurous, well traveled, and—with the presidency of JFK—has a full head of hair. He is young. (Somehow FDR and Wilson are remembered as if they were always young in high office.)

In the age of ceaseless media scrutiny, the mythical American president looks increasingly absurd. Poor Jimmy Carter was exhausted by the end of his first year in office with all the phony values the role demanded of him. The requisite athleticism caused him to pass out in an ill-considered public marathon and to beat an alleged killer rabbit with a canoe paddle. His attempts at the hearty laugh aroused mistrust among millions who perceived it as an idiot grin. Governor Dukakis's efforts landed him in an Army tank with what looked like a football helmet on his tiny head. Actually, from 1992 to the present, the accumulating burden of false pieties, silly poses, and bogus values undid every Democratic presidential candidate but Bill Clinton. Only Clinton was sufficiently plastic and sufficiently the impostor to ape them all without blowing up.

Hillary might also have what it takes to become the first female mythical American president. She is intellectual, arty, well traveled, adventurous, and always on the underdog's side. Being athletic could present a problem for her, yet her flabby mama's boy of a husband managed it despite the fact that his biographies are full of anecdotes about how the jocks back in Arkansas razzed him in the locker room. As for youthfulness, she can always lie about her age. Although her hair was problematic in her White House days, causing her to run through scores of appalling coifs, she now seems to have turned hair into a major strength—if we are to believe her memoir. The bit about having a hearty laugh, however, will always be insurmountable for Hillary. When she laughs, observers have noticed, her eyes do not move.

If the Democratic rank and file are particularly susceptible to the presidential myths fashioned for them by their mythmakers in the

Kultursmog, the Democratic candidates have been striving mightily to embody these myths. When Vice President Al Gore jogged and joshed, carried books under his arm in Campaign 2000, and embellished his biography with phony war stories from Vietnam and high-tech prodigies on the Senate floor, he was derided as a hoaxer, unable to decide on his wardrobe. After the last votes in Campaign 2000 were cast or miscast or not cast at all, the poor guy was kissed off as a poor loser. In 2003, Senator John Kerry became pathetic in a hilarious way, claiming to be an intellectual, a regular guy, a poet, a guitar player, "the Primal John," reported the *Washington Post,* "the pilot who flies barrel rolls, who relaxes by windsurfing in a squall, who ran with the bulls at Pamplona and, when trampled, got up, chased the bull, and grabbed for its horns." *Do not* even ask to what primal purpose he put those horns.[3] He is very rich and very kind, a patron of the arts, possessed of handsome, sculpted features—sculpted, admittedly, by cosmetic surgeons but surgeons with a sense of history, surgeons devoted to delivering to their client a majestic chin (yes, his chin is one of his proudest achievements), the kind of chin that would lead nations and calm troubled waters. Thus arrived this candidate of the outthrust chin who can elicit trust from the masses, would fain boast of his war record and of his opposition to the Iraq war, of his stupendous health and of his prostate operation. Before the first primary he had discovered that he was a Jew, though on faraway St. Patrick Days he had bragged that he was Irish. He got into a snit with the Bush White House whose agents claimed he looked French. He publicly denied it. The campaign rollicked on. In desperation I half expected him to undertake bungee jumps and skydiving.

It is arguably the sheer weight of the mythical baggage that Democrats have brought down on their candidates through the years that has made these candidates so unpersuasive in presidential elections. Since FDR (who was spared the need to be a jock), Bill Clinton is the only recent Democrat who has won two presidential terms, though doing so necessitated his filching Republican policies and implicating independent counsel Ken Starr in a *coup d'etat*. The sorry fact is that lesser candidates attempting to affect the burgeoning values of the mythical American presidency end up looking so bizarre that the average American voter does not want to have him in the White House or as a next-door neighbor. (Actually, I doubt ordinary Americans would want the Clintons living next door. Living behind iron gates in a large white house in a non-residential neighborhood in the District of Columbia was fine with the electorate so long as the economy was vibrant and no one knew about the terrorists whom the president only occasionally hosted. Who in the Heartland would want such a menagerie nearby?)

Fortunately for Clinton, the Democratic mythmakers have never made character an important value for the mythical American presidency, possibly because the mythmakers themselves are in dispute as to character's ingredients. Clinton's famously shabby character did cause that issue to arise in both of his elections, but, given the peace and prosperity of the time, the electorate never paid much attention to the problems caused by the Clintons' scandals, and many relished the personal drama that really was unsurpassed. Thus the Democratic mythmakers took what they could from his supposedly log-cabin upbringing and created what might someday be seen as the last example of the mythical American president. Many place him right in the line that extends from TR to JFK.

From Theodore Roosevelt to his sixth cousin, Franklin, and on to John F. Kennedy, the mythmakers have been bequeathed ever more meager raw material from which to craft their mythic figures. From Kennedy to Clinton the material changed from sand to sawdust—not that the mythmakers' efforts have slackened. In fact, their feats have grown Herculean, to wondrously comic effect. Consider Sidney Blumenthal's priceless evocation of his master, Boy Clinton. It perfectly demonstrates the evolutionary delirium of the *Kultursmog*'s mythical American president. Writes Blumenthal in his fantasy-ridden memoir, *The Clinton Wars:* "Just as the presidents of the late twentieth century operated in the shadow of FDR, those of the first part of the twenty-first century will stand in the shadow of Clinton."[4] One wonders what lewd acts Blumer expects Clinton's successors to be perpetrating in those shadows. Will the cops be called in? Will hounds howl through the night and cats knock over garbage cans?

The two heroic presidents whom Blumenthal assumes labored in FDR's shadow, JFK and Clinton, achieved nothing comparable to FDR's achievements either in foreign or domestic policy. In fact, aside from charm, they have little in common with FDR, though they shared a quality peculiar to the modern Democratic presidency: sexual recklessness. Lyndon Johnson had a tendency for this sort of spur-of-the-moment coitus, too; but most historians leave that rock unturned. Old Beagle-Ears, for whatever reason, has few adulators in the *Kultursmog*.

As a young World War II naval officer, JFK had a long and passionate affair with Inga Arvad, a woman believed by the FBI and historians such as Thomas C. Reeves to have been personally commissioned by Adolf Hitler to spy on the United States. Years later, he was involved with Ellen Rometsch, a woman suspected of being an agent for East German intelligence. While in the White House he shared a woman, Judith Exner, with one of the country's most powerful mafiosi, Sam Giancana, entangling his most intimate confidences with organized crime. He had an affair with Marilyn Monroe, who was suicidally unstable and apparently willing to embarrass the president publicly. On one occasion, he paraded prostitutes past families who had turned out to cheer him on a military base. Surely during a life of carnal marathons JFK entertained hundreds of less controversial cuties. Four decades after his assassination, Americans learned that their thirty-fifth president even had his own White House intern, Marion "Mimi" Fahnestock.

The names of Clinton's reckless sex contacts are well known, and by the time historians and journalists have picked over his chaotic little black books and followed the plenitude of tips they will get over the years the list will lengthen. I can report that at the *American Spectator* we knew and interviewed five other White House interns Clinton was availing himself of. Yet there is a difference between Clinton's scandals and those of JFK, a difference that shows how Blumenthal's mythical American president has deteriorated even from JFK. Underlings always tattled on Clinton. They never did on Kennedy. Bodyguards, cooks, nannies, and low-level political aides went to the press about Clinton. The same class of people witnessed Kennedy's revelries, but they never snitched. The reason is that Kennedy, even with his pants down, apparently had a dignity that escapes Clinton both in private and in public. Kennedy's underlings recognized him as a gentleman. There is little evidence of him treating his staff badly. But both Clintons have mistreated staff for years, as abundant reports testify. Their boorishness has inspired little loyalty from anyone save those who received the high-end glamour jobs and preferment.

The Arkansas troopers, nannies, government bureaucrats, and political aides who talked to me about Clinton simply did not respect him. In fact, many of those whom I interviewed betrayed an amused contempt for both Clintons as they cited the nasty side of Madame Hillary and the coarseness of the Boy President. No aide, servant, or friend of JFK whom I ever knew lacked respect for the president. Old Arthur Krock, a friend of JFK's father and a distinguished *New York Times* columnist, once confided to me that "the Kennedy boys were so very shallow," but that is about as rude a remark from a Kennedy confidant as I ever heard. Of both Clintons I heard mostly disdain.

Bill's bodyguards spoke more of his coarseness and selfishness than of anything else; evidence of these traits was forever popping up in public. Clinton may be charming, but he is no gentleman, and his wife rarely acted the part of a lady until she became Senator Clinton. Both, in their dealings with aides high and low and in their conduct of the nation's business, proceeded without dignity. They made egregious demands on those around them, turning guards into pimps and government employees into nannies, comfort women, and errand runners. That is why the scandal stories arose from their own subordinates.

I had my own personal encounter with Bill's adolescent nature in Washington's Jockey Club, when he sought to pacify me with his reputed charm and gift for small talk. In *Boy Clinton* I record the amazing moment. Having just written a story about how Clinton, in the mid-1980s, involved an Arkansas state trooper in a federal government operation to supply arms to the *contras* in Central America, I was curious as to his response. The operation had been mentioned in the left-wing press for years. It was a CIA initiative that got entangled in drug trafficking after the agency employed an ex-drug trafficker to fly the planes, not an infrequent problem in those sorts of clandestine operations. My contribution to the story was that Clinton was aware of the flights going out of a rural Arkansas airport, though what he had known about the drugs coming back into the country remains uncertain. At our *tête-à-tête* that night in the Jockey Club, I asked him about the story. Surrounded by Secret Service guards, he went into one of the towering rages for which he is famous. What I remember most about his diatribe was that it combined indignant rebuke with childish whines. It was rage was without force of character. Moreover, he, the president of the United States, just kept repeating his pitiable complaints. It fell to me, the writer, to end the display. I told him, "Mr. President, we can continue this later. You have guests waiting for you at your table." One was Hillary, and the glare she was giving me was more alarming than her husband's tirade.

The mythmakers have chosen to transform this Boy President into their latest giant. His ignominious impeachment has been mined for one more installment of the mythical American president saga. In the end, his wholly unnecessary—if he had done the honorable thing and resigned—impeachment has been portrayed in the *Kultursmog* as a heroic defense of the Constitution against a power grab by radical Republicans.

For decades, Clinton had charmed his liberal professors and the Democratic elders while mastering the false pieties and bogus values the *Kultursmog*'s myth machine required: the polymathic intellect with the homespun touch and all the silly attitudinizing that goes with it. Add the capacious intellect and the big heart, the story of the man from Hope, Arkansas: the boy who had stood up to an abusive, alcoholic stepfather and risen to the heights of the liberals' meritocracy. When this eternal boy mounted the podium as a candidate, with his engaging smile and pompadour of silver hair, he was the mythmakers' dream, a Kennedy among the hillbillies, a mythical American president whose shadow Sidney Blumenthal perceived looming over the twenty-first century.

Some of the fondest wishes of the mythmakers turn out to be true. Clinton did govern as a centrist. He stood for a big hike in the minimum wage, but he was also willing to cut capital gains taxes. He was for large grants to urban communities, but he also professed an eagerness for welfare reform, which he signed after a Republican Congress forced it on him. He was the candidate, as all Democrats are, of the labor unions, but once in office he did an about-face and became eager to complete the North American Free Trade Agreement and other free-trade deals for the business sector of the United States.

This centrism was in keeping with his political savior Dick Morris's scheme called "triangulation," that is, playing one's own party against the opposition. Clinton had no original economic policy of his own. While he ostentatiously signed legislation that sounded like a grand economic plan, it was based on no economic model, as, say, supply-side economics is based on a model. Its only strategy was political, and Clinton showed no interest in the plan's economic details. After all, it was essentially an amalgam of the same Reagan-Bush economics he had run against in 1992. All it represented for him was a tool of Morris's triangulation plan, the scheme to save his floundering presidency.

Morris had performed Governor Clinton's resuscitation in Arkansas after Hillary's left-wing schemes nearly cost Bill his political life. Morris returned in the mid-1990s to save Clinton's presidency from Hillary's left-wing excesses. In pursuit of Morris's scheme, Clinton had but to continue, in moderated form, the economic policies that he had denounced in 1992 as the cause of a recession that verged upon "depression"—when it was actually the mildest recession in decades. For all the sound and fury over Clinton's early tax increases, eventually dramatic cuts were made in the capital gains tax and home equity was treated more fairly, both of which had originated as GOP policies. During Clinton's administration, federal spending remained a relatively low percentage of GDP, largely due to continued increases in national wealth. Federal employment declined through attrition and through savage and shortsighted defense cuts.

To compensate for his larcenous appropriation of Republican economic policies, Clinton had to portray himself as a hero who moderated the vicious instincts of the beastly Republicans. This was the other side of triangulation—a side that Hillary relished: demonizing the opposition. Bill Clinton had to become the indispensable Democrat, resolute in standing up to Republican ideologues. He had to become the defender of the rule of law, portraying the Republicans as anarchists and zealots.

The fact remains, however, that Clinton's centrism was forced on him by Hillary's left-wing excesses in the first two years of the administration. After campaigning in 1992 as a moderate, Clinton allowed himself a sharp veer to the left, orchestrated mostly by the Hillary section of the West Wing—the attempt to centralize health care, the attempt to turn crime legislation into midnight basketball, the gays-in-the-military issue. All this struck the American people as a betrayal; they responded with the Republican mid-term victories of 1994. The American people were angered and alarmed that such a seemingly centrist Democrat had permitted his agenda to make such a leftward lurch. They retaliated by ending Democratic dominance on Capitol Hill, in governors' mansions, and in state legislatures.

There were, of course, other factors at work behind the 1994 debacle—the memory of the House banking scandal was fresh, and senior Democrats were filmed sunning themselves on Caribbean beaches while on "fact-finding missions." Going back thirty years, the Democratic majority in the House, once the legacy of the New Deal, had radicalized after the election of a new, leftist Watergate class. But the issue that famously galvanized the revolt against the Democrats was the Hillary health care monstrosity. It brought down the House.

Once a Republican majority was in control of the House of Representatives, the president found that his attempt at triangulation had resulted in an isosceles triangle with long Republican sides and a narrowing base, where the angle pinched Clinton in the Democratic corner. As the scandals mounted, the President had to invest more of his political capital in Republican programs just to survive. And so he signed welfare reform and tax relief into law, in a form much closer to the ideals of Newt Gingrich and Tom DeLay than those of Marian Wright Edelman and George McGovern.

"He called us all together, and spread out all the things he wanted to achieve in his second term," confides one former Clinton aide who recalls the president's morose behavior during the impeachment debacle. "We talked it through, and he was the one who brought us to the realization that there was very little we could do. The president had big plans, but there was no room to maneuver. And he had no one but himself to blame."

Another political party might have ditched Clinton, publicly urging him to resign to spare the nation the ordeal of impeachment. It is difficult to imagine Republican support remaining solid if Ronald Reagan or George H.W. Bush had made such poor use of an office intern and then lied about it, had appeared before a grand jury and lied again, and had finally been forced to come clean before the nation on such a sordid subject. There were sound reasons for the Democrats to prevail on Clinton to pull a Nixon and simply resign. The resignation would have put Al Gore in position to run in 2000 as an incumbent. Given the closeness of that election, is there any doubt that the power of incumbency would have given President Gore the necessary votes in Florida to have sewn it up?

Surely Democratic leaders understood these calculations, but they stood by Clinton to a degree that Republicans never stood by Nixon. Recent American history has shown that of the two parties, the Democrats are what we might call the fighting party. They defend their own when their own are in trouble. When a Democratic member of Congress is caught with his hand in the till or in an unmentionable place, the Democrats close ranks. When the same sort of contretemps befalls a Republican, he is on his own. The Hon. Barney Frank, after declaring his homosexuality, suffered through the scandal of a police investigation that revealed that his boyfriend was running a sex service out of the congressman's Washington residence. The Hon. Frank is with us still and honored among Democrats. A Republican solon's scandals are usually less ridiculous. Nonetheless, they rarely go unpunished by fellow Republicans, after which Republican voters usually vote them out. In the 1980s, both Congressman Gerry Studds, a Democrat, and Dan Crane, a Republican, were censured for having sexual relations with seventeen-year-old congressional pages, Studds with a boy, Crane with a girl. Studds's career went on, untroubled by constituent protest. Crane's Republican constituency rejected him at the next election. Or recall what we might see as a Republican prelude to Clinton's impeachment. In 1995, when the number of women harassed by the Kissing Senator, Robert Packwood, hit a critical mass, he, a Republican moderate (and proud feminist!), was forced to resign with no fellow Republican around to hold his coat.

Three years later, when Boy Clinton was impeached for brazen mis-
behavior involving sex, perjury, and obstruction of justice, the Democratic Party stood by him, to its long-term discredit but to Clinton's
relief.

In getting drawn into the impeachment debacle, many Democrats
still brag about their performance as if it were a victory. Nowhere in
their celebrations does it seem to dawn on them how pathetic and pal-
try and pyrrhic their victory was.

Consider the victories of past presidents. FDR drove the dominant
Republican Party into minority status for two generations, changed
the direction of American policy in foreign and domestic affairs, and
won a world war. Harry Truman founded NATO and the Marshall
Plan while consolidating the New Deal. Dwight D. Eisenhower
ensured that America remained internationalist, pursued the Cold
War, and established the interstate highway system. Richard Nixon
went to China. Jimmy Carter brought peace between Israel and Egypt.
Ronald Reagan achieved his predecessor FDR's feat in redirecting
American foreign and domestic policy, and he also won the Cold War.
George H.W. Bush assembled an extraordinary international coalition
and achieved a smashing victory to liberate Kuwait from the tyranny
of Saddam Hussein.

And what has been the Clinton achievement? He managed to
survive—and in some instances, turn the tables on—a succession of
floozies and low-level whistle-blowers. He managed to cling to power
by his fingernails and stay out of the hoosegow, thanks to an array of
high-powered Washington lawyers. Never before has a first couple
been so personally engaged in so many contests of will and credibility against the likes of Gennifer Flowers, Paula Jones, the McDougals,
and all the buffoons en train with Monica Lewinsky. Despite this

tawdriness, Clinton remains secure in the Democrats' hall of presidential myth. When President Clinton staged his long "power" walk down the corridor to the stage of the Democratic National Convention in 2000, he demonstrated just how far gone the Democratic Party is on its mythopoeic fantasies.

Democrats in Denial

The final outcome of the Clinton administration came as a surprise to just about every political observer unaware of the Clintons' prior record in Arkansas.

This was not how the Clinton presidency should have turned out. Bill Clinton's election followed six years in which Republicans had lost momentum and coherence. It was a downward spiral that had started with the Republicans' loss of the Senate in 1986. This loss, in turn, allowed the Democrats to use Senate investigative powers to pursue the distractions of the Iran-Contra investigations, creating a melancholy end to the otherwise triumphant Reagan presidency. The decline continued under President George H.W. Bush, who was so publicly mauled by Senate Democratic leader George Mitchell that he scarcely dared to present a domestic agenda. By the time the Clintons arrived in Washington, they were poised to lead a Democratic renaissance.

At that time, the Grand Old Party had become a ship becalmed in a political Dead Sea. As soon as Hillary began to talk of health care, however, the sails of the Republican hulk begin to rustle. The more she talked, the more those sails billowed. The more she schemed, the faster the Grand Old Party began to cut through the water, sailing as it had not done in years, not even at the height of the Reagan era.

It might be difficult to recall now, but a Democratic clique of congressional *exaltés* governed Washington in the early 1990s. Les Aspin, a gentle man in a sweater with a dog by his fireplace, dominated defense policy in Congress before making a mess of it in the Pentagon. Tom Foley, lanky and sententious, presided as Speaker of the House. And, of course, there was the grandest of the *exaltés*, Dan Rostenkowski, who as chairman of the Ways and Means Committee had seen presidents come and go, often matching them in power.

Under Clinton, all these powerful men were brought to political (and in some cases, personal) ruin. You can argue that the collapse of the congressional barons and the Republican takeover of the House were a long time coming. You can argue that the Republicans, once free of the senior Bush, were allowed to tap into the powerful energies of their ideas.

There is no doubt, however, that Hillary's radical proposal to centralize health care was the ultimate cause of the collapse of a Democratic majority that had ruled for almost the entire postwar period. For decades, the Democrats had stayed in power by allowing conservative members from the South and West to publicly cast their votes against liberal programs while privately upholding the passage of those programs by sustaining the liberals' grip on House rules. Discipline was enforced by whips and by secret ballots in the Democratic caucus, which approved chairmanships. You might be a blue dog Democrat from Lubbock, but if you crossed the liberal leadership of the House you might as well have gone back to being a city councilman.

This sort of subterfuge changed when the Democrats had to scramble for floor votes. "The spectacle of Democrats passing their budget and tax increases by one-vote margins in the House and Senate reduced to zero the credibility of Democratic incumbents who said they were moderates but who voted with the leadership," writes Michael Barone. The defeat of the liberal 1994 crime package—larded with pork and seasoned with social programs—publicly exposed the mechanism. On top of this, Hillary's 1,300-page health care plan was simply too much. It landed on this politically fragile structure like a flying anvil.[5] "A clearer repudiation of the party in power cannot be imagined," Barone concluded. "Wherever history is headed, it is no longer headed left."[6]

President Clinton probably recognized the danger signs. His political instincts have always been keener than those of his wife. He tried to moderate Madame Hillary's proposal to socialize health care. But his past indiscretions had put him in Hillary's vise. One prominent Western Democrat observed at the time, "Clinton seems to be waffling. . . . He puts out this 95 percent, and Hillary says, 'No, universal coverage,' and all of a sudden Bill's saying, 'Yeah, universal coverage.' It's like she hit him over the head with a fry pan."[7]

The Democrats have suffered a precipitous drop from the commanding majorities of the 1970s, accompanied by a startling fall from power. Much of this has to be blamed on the declining appeal of liberalism, but much of the blame also resides with the Clintons, who exposed the essential insincerity of the Democratic approach to governing.

Before the Clintons, the Democratic Party held power.

THE HOUSE OF REPRESENTATIVES

Congress	Cycle	Democrats	Republicans
89	1965–1966	295	140
94	1975–1976	291	144
102	1991–1992	267	167
103	1993–1994	258	176

Then came the year of Hillary and health care:

104	1995–1996	204	230

In the 1960s and 1970s, the Democrats thrice hit a high-water mark of more than 290 members (out of a total of 435).

The Reagan years had whittled them down a bit. But Democrats were still enjoying monolithic control of the House when Bill Clinton came to office. Then, in the aftermath of Hillary Rodham Clinton's health care debacle, the House Democrats lost fifty-two seats, and a Republican became speaker for the first time in forty years.

The Clintons' apologists claim that they were able to reverse this trend—and, to be fair, there was some backsliding for the rest of the decade. Newt Gingrich and the Republicans engaged Clinton in a game of chicken over the government shutdown. Then they lost their nerve. Gingrich proved to be a masterful agitator—the Contract with America was a brilliant piece of agitprop—but at governing he was inept. He lost his bearings. At times, Gingrich seemed more interested in co-authoring novels or imparting his theories of history to graduate students than in managing the House. In another example of the *Kultursmog*'s politically polluted condition, the Republicans' "revolution" rhetoric was condemned as "extremism." I can think of no liberal Democratic initiative that has ever been termed as "extremism." The Clintons exploited the Oklahoma bombing and successfully claimed that it was consanguineous with this Republican "revolution." Gingrich did not have the wit to oppose the Clintons' perverse comparisons of Republicans and Rush Limbaugh to Timothy McVeigh.

What is remarkable is that the Republican majority sustained all this damage and still retained control. For all its faults, the Republican House majority has proved remarkably durable. Trends in demographics, reapportionment, and retirements now cause Democratic insiders, as well as Republicans, to project that the GOP will easily continue its House rule. "We'll be out of power for a decade," confides one Democratic fund-raiser.

A similar trend can be seen in the Senate, in which the disastrous middle years of the Clinton administration generated a transformation in American politics.

THE SENATE

Congress	Cycle	Democrats	Republicans
89	1965–1966	68	32
103	1993–1994	57	43

Then came the year of Hillary and health care:

104	1995–1996	48	52
105	1997–1998	45	55

Senate Democrats were able to bring themselves back in control for a brief period during the early George W. Bush administration, mainly through death and a defection in the Republican ranks. They have held their own only by straining for victory; witness the corrupt senator Robert Torricelli's last-minute retirement from the New Jersey Senate race in favor of a more electable substitute. But the long-term trends look very unpromising for Democrats hoping to retake the Senate.

State Legislatures

A similar pattern can be seen in state legislatures, the farm league of American politics.

Year	Democratic Control	Republican Control	Split
1974	37	4	8
1992	25	8	16

Then came the year of Hillary and health care:

Year	Democratic Control	Republican Control	Split
1994	18	19	12

Governors

Democrats had seen a marked growth in their gubernatorial prospects, with more incumbents in Southern and Western states. Even here, though, the "Hillary effect" is pronounced—a sudden plunge after 1994.

Year	Democrats	Republicans	Ind.
1974	32	18	0
1990	29	21	0
1991	29	19	2
1992	28	20	2
1993	30	18	2

After the year of Hillary and health care:

Year	Democrats	Republicans	Ind.
1995	19	30	1

In each instance—from the House to the Senate to the states—1994 was the signal year, the one in which Americans decided that the Democratic Party was just too liberal to govern. The subsequent impeachment debacle prompted James Carville to write an apologia, *Stickin': The Case for Loyalty*. The problem was, under the Clintons it was the Democratic Party itself that wound up getting stuck. On the whole, sticking with the Clintons was costing the Democrats dearly.

Through the year 2000, the Democrats continued to pay a dispendious price for their loyalty to the Clintons, and the Democrat who paid the highest price was the Clintons' loyal sidekick, Vice President Al Gore. Running on an eight-year record of peace and prosperity, Vice President Gore should have won the presidency in 2000 as handily as Vice President George H. W. Bush had in 1988, but Gore suffered the Clinton schizophrenia in 2000, which added to his general implausibility. He, who in the immediate aftermath of impeachment called Clinton "one of our greatest presidents," squirmed over the scabrous Clinton record during Campaign 2000. A squirmer is not a leader. It was not just Gore's evasions, his ever-changing campaign strategies, and his Jekyll and Hyde performances in the debates that undid him in 2000; it was his schizoid relationship with "one of our greatest presidents."

Hillary's senatorial race displayed another aspect of the burden that the Clintons had become for Democrats. The *New Republic* editorialized presciently in 1999 when it mused, "She could divert resources from other candidates, politicize their races in ways that don't play well beyond the Upper West Side, and become a rallying point for conservatives still itching to exploit anti-Clinton sentiment. She could, in other words, do precisely what her husband has done time and again—sacrifice the good of her party and her cause to satisfy her own ambitions."[8]

Democrats worried that Hillary's senatorial campaign might energize the Republican base, assist the Republican fund-raisers, and get out the Republican vote. Waggish commentators predicted that she would be the leading fund-raiser for both the Republican and the Democratic parties.

The central legacy is clear. The Clintons were—and remain—a burden to their party. Hillary's victory in New York was no help to the Democrats. And the presence of both Clintons on the national stage seems to help only them. "The Clintons suck up every bit of the available air," complains Susan Estrich. "Nothing is left for anyone else. They are big, too big. That's the problem. . . ."[9]

CHAPTER SEVEN

The Presidency of Clinton 44

"There can be no such thing as a successful traitor,
for if one succeeds he becomes a founding father."[1]

—Saul Alinsky

DESPITE THE POLITICAL DRAG the Clintons exert on their fellow Democrats, Hillary, paradoxically, remains the party's nominee-in-waiting for some future bid for the presidency. Once nominated, Hillary only needs one stroke of good luck to win—the good luck of facing yet another bad Republican campaign (like that of Bush senior in 1992). What would it be like to have Hillary Rodham Clinton as president? Consider how it might begin: A fictitious memo. . .

· · · · ·

1/1/2009

TO: HRC

FROM: Linda Bloodworth-Thomason

RE: Inauguration Day/A Treatment

CONCEPT: The "Reality" Inaugural

Reality TV works by positioning tiny cameras at multiple angles along the pathway of an event, heightening drama and creating a "movie-like" feel. This was done to dramatize the arrival of President Clinton in his long "power walk" to the stage of the 2000 Democratic convention. The time has come to transform the drab public-service spectacle of the Presidential Inauguration.

SCENE: THE ARRIVAL

January in Washington. Zinc clouds low over the Capitol. Crowds braving the frigid weather, gamely waving flags all along Pennsylvania Avenue.

CUT: President George W. Bush and Laura stand on the portico, politely waiting for the arrival of the President-Elect, and for the era of Republican dominance to end—replicating the scene in 1992 in which Bill had wrested the presidency from Bush's father.

CUT: The armored Cadillac bearing HRC and Bill Clinton comes to an abrupt halt. The door opens just as a young U.S. Marine snaps a salute. HRC/POTUS-elect emerges in a tailored

Donna Karan suit—something dark blue, with a bold, baby-blue "power tie" fashioned from a scarf (no Hermès, domestic only pleeze!). Tie it in the fashion of a cravat.

[Note: Walk fast, stay ahead of Bill!]

TRACKING SHOT: HRC boldly strides up the carpeted stairs to briskly shake the hands of the Bushes. Smile broadly, as if old friends.

CUT to successive shots of Bushes leading Clintons through White House. Expect a hoary joke from President Bush, "Guess I don't have to show you around the joint, now do I?" Retire upstairs, where RESIDENCE-CAM picks up the two couples sitting at a divan, Laura pouring tea. Graciously accept a cup but immediately set it down.

Pretend to be engrossed in small talk and proffered advice from the last Bush to ever occupy the White House. No sound from the residence will be overheard during this period, allowing for thoughtful commentators like Paul Begala and James Carville to offer their thoughts from little inset boxes on the screen.

CUT to LIMO-CAM: Inside of presidential limousine. Put on that thousand-watt smile and those high-beam eyes while waving at the crowd. Try to create a contrast with W. With any luck, he'll scowl, making him look like another Herbert Hoover and you like another Roosevelt. Exude optimism. Think Franklin. Think Eleanor!

CUT to presidential party exiting limo under the stands in the front of the Capitol, following party to the podium and introductions. (With reality TV, we can finally dispense with the dead air time of senators and judges and their families waiting in the cold, blowing their noses, smoothing their hair, and whispering jokes to one another.)

Shake the hands of George and Barbara Bush, wide smile of recognition—again, as if they were old friends. Cast a quick admiring glance at soon-to-be-former President Bush—no longer than 2.5 seconds.

MEDIUM-CLOSE UP of swearing-in. Take it slow, look the chief justice in the eye, repeat every word with conviction, and hit "so help me God" with rising emphasis.

Don't let your hands waver, either on the Bible or your raised hand in the air. Visualize yourself as immutable, planted.

THE SPEECH

Every inaugural speech notes the miracle of the uninterrupted and peaceful transfer of the world's most powerful office. Reflect on that, then make the obligatory nod to your predecessor, offering Bush a compliment so pallid that it will be forgotten before he can even nod in acknowledgement.

Say a special word about your husband and his valuable counsel. That will allow you to segue into the specialness of this election. Reach for the high tone, think JFK! Something like this . . .

"From the founding of the Republic until the early twentieth century, one half of America's talent, one half of America's vision, one half of America's potential leadership was excluded from high office—America's women—kept even from their right to vote.

"For almost another century, the women of America pioneered their abilities and responsibilities, only to find a glass ceiling was keeping them from attaining the highest responsibilities of all.

"Today, that glass ceiling has been shattered. I am here to tell every girl in America that one day she may grow up to become President . . . because this girl did."

• Be sure to quote Abigail Adams and Eleanor Roosevelt.

• Quickly get to foreign policy—echo the Kennedy hard line on communism, applying it to terrorism. Doing so will clear the way to get to the real meat of the speech—domestic policy.

Health Care

Talk about the need for a rich nation to finally assume its responsibilities to take care of the weakest and most vulnerable. Do not use the words "universal access"—it scares people. You've learned this lesson!

Taxes

Don't jump into the briar patch of openly opposing the past administration's tax cuts. Instead, talk in abstract terms of matching our means to our programs. The time to propose a huge tax increase can come later, in the spring.

Wrap-Up: Talk Values and Meaning

"The primal story of America was of a people struggling to build their own land of freedom—to dig fields out of virgin forests, to transform fallow ground into fertile farms, to end slavery and overcome our own racism, to win two world wars and be the first to the moon. The twenty-first century finds us a nation transformed and facing new challenges our forebears could never have imagined.

"Now we are a people of plenty—a nation overloaded with food and luxuries, yet hungry for consequential work. We are a people whose daily lives are minutely scheduled, yet lacking any time to reflect on the purpose of all this business. We are people entertained in a hundred ways, yet yearning in the silent hours of the night for an injection of meaning into our lives.

"America grew to greatness under the New Deal. We touched the world through the New Frontier. Now I promise you a presidency devoted to the New Meaning."

Conclude by implying that Americans will find meaning in the great undertakings of a new and energetic administration.

Final note: A study of past inaugurals shows that this time in January is typically cloudy, with the weather scattering in the afternoon. With any luck, the clouds will break before the end of your speech, opening a shaft of golden light like a benediction. Just to be sure we have that light, we might procure one of those slow-moving Predator drones from the Coalition forces in Iraq and have it shoot a harmless golden laser beam to the crown of your head.

· · · · ·

The Great Deception

Madame Hillary would, in her wildest dreams, undoubtedly relish a presidency that was an unending left-wing rampage, a national Cambodian re-education camp for anyone caught wearing an Adam Smith necktie or scarf. Such "extremists" are the enemy, after all, composing the Vast Right-Wing Conspiracy that must be scotched if Clintonian America is to be saved. She would install an all-woman Cabinet to thumb her nose at the patriarchy. (After all, one of the prices Hillary exacted from Bill in 1992 was the appointment of a female attorney general and, later, a female secretary of state.) With Hillary now making all the appointments, why not have a Cabinet full of short-haired harridans and crypto-Marxists from assorted left-wing hothouses? Why not have an entire administration of nominees like Dr. Johnetta Cole, Hillary's first choice for secretary of education in 1992, who had backed Cuban intervention in Angola and publicly broke with Joan Baez and other former anti-Vietnam War activists over the persecution of 400,000 political prisoners? "Should they not be reeducated?" Dr. Coles asked.

"Hillary is the ideologue, the true-blue leftist," said one Arkansas politician who has known them for years. "Bill Clinton is far more willing to compromise. The rap on him in Arkansas is that he couldn't hold a grudge. She's the strident one, the partisan one."[2] Welcome to Camp Hillary. Please remove your glasses and deposit them on the heap. (Was that a flash of gold I saw in your teeth?)

In short, if Hillary Clinton is elected, conservatives, who understand what she would do if she could, might be ready to plant a "for sale" sign in front of the house, pack their belongings, and sprint to the airport. (Though, of course, at the airport they'd find that there's no place to go; the left's *Kultursmog* has, worse than any other form of pollution, drifted over the entire western world).

But if conservatives take heart, they can impose barriers against Madame Hillary's agenda similar to those they were able to impose against the depredations of the Billary years. Bill Clinton let slip a few left-wing wacko nominations (remember Surgeon General Joycelyn Elders, the proponent of masturbation, and Lani Guinier?). But they caused him so much trouble that he learned to be at least a bit more cautious, and, in reality, seemed to consider the more left-wing appointments as a sop to the left wing of his party so he could have the freedom to govern from the center. Hillary will have the opposite problem. She is the dauphine of the left. She will have to prove to the rest of America that she can be trusted. Therefore, one should expect to see her fill her Cabinet with solid, gray, establishment Democrats. Expect to see Jennifer Granholm, the promising governor of Michigan, in an important job. Expect to see Evan Bayh, telegenic senator from Indiana, military leaders like Wesley Clark, and the return of respected wisemen (Lee Hamilton, Sam Nunn) who always win the tepid, good-government plaudits of writers like David Broder of the *Washington Post*. And, of course, there will be one or two Clinton Republicans after the fashion of Clinton's secretary of defense, William Cohen.

Expect, too, to see little-known members of Hillary's Senate staff in powerful White House jobs. One of them will surely be Tamera Luzzatto, a Harvard-educated aide to Senator John D. "Jay" Rockefeller, IV, who is well regarded by Republicans and Democrats alike in her service as Hillary's Senate chief of staff.

Expect to see Ann O'Leary, former Clinton administration aide who monitors legislation and policy for Hillary, along with deputy chief of staff Kris Balderston, the former Clinton White House aide whose experience in government dates back to serving Governor Michael Dukakis. Media maven Howard Wolfson, Hillary's favorite punching bag in the election, will likely be back for more punishment. (He is an aerophobe who will have to get over his fear of flying if he wants to be part of a national campaign.) Philippe Reines, Hillary's D.C. press secretary, is young and regarded by the press as still earning his stripes. All of them are highly talented. They will make the cut to the West Wing.

Hillary's closest aides are two women largely unknown to most of Washington, Patti Solis Doyle and Kelly Craighead. Of the two, Solis Doyle is the most powerful. The daughter of Mexican immigrants, she learned politics and government while working for Chicago mayor Richard M. Daley. A former White House aide, she oversaw logistics and helped on campaign strategy in Hillary's Senate race. Solis Doyle now holds the keys to the kingdom, running HILLPAC and overseeing much of the labyrinthine world of Hillary's interlocking campaign committees. Hillary's other close aide, Craighead, is a striking blonde, as poised in high-pressure social situations as she was on the high board when she trained as a competitive diver in California. Craighead has a reputation as a talented event planner. In *Living History*, Hillary recounts the story of the Queen Mother being so charmed by

Craighead on the royal yacht *Britannia* that she asked her to stay for dinner. "Her black pantsuit wouldn't do," Hillary writes. "I pulled out all my dressy clothes and helped Kelly piece together a suitable outfit for dining with the Queen Mother."[3] In the political world, such people are gold.

In short, the public face of the next Clinton administration can be expected to be professional, balanced between the sexes, apparently moderate, competent, and benign. Do not expect to see Susan Thomases as attorney general or Harold Ickes reprising his father's New Deal role as secretary of the interior. In short, do not expect to turn on your television and see the scarecrow faces of the hard left.

But they will be there nevertheless. The more powerful ones, like Ickes, will play an outside role. The real work will be done, however, by effective leftists safely and securely placed in powerful jobs that are out of the public view. This will be the great Hillary deception: the world of Senator Hillary presented to the public, the world of Madame Hillary working away in jobs out of the limelight that really matter. Washington insiders know that the real work in the government is done not by the Cabinet secretaries, but by the second- and third-tier people, the assistant secretaries and the deputy assistant secretaries. It is into these positions that Hillary will quietly salt the departments and agencies with the true believers, the people dedicated to making irreversible decisions that will lock America on to the path of social control.

Most alarming of all is to consider the enhanced powers the next President Clinton would inherit. In the last Clinton administration, we saw the frequency with which conservative groups and critics were hit with IRS audits. In the mid-1990s, an honor role of conservative organizations—ranging from the Heritage Foundation to the

National Rifle Association—found themselves defending their books against the Feds. The *Washington Times* investigated and found no similar range of audits among liberal groups.

The audits extended to individuals, for instance, Paula Corbin Jones, who got her call from the IRS after she refused to settle her sexual harassment suit in a way the Clintons deemed agreeable. After Kent Masterson Brown filed a lawsuit forcing Hillary Clinton to open up the secret deliberations of her health care committee, he too was audited. So was Billy Dale, the unlucky White House travel office director whose misfortune was to be in a position that the Clintons wanted to fill when they first arrived at 1600 Pennsylvania Avenue. Not to put too fine a point on all this IRS activity, but the *Washington Times* also reported that in the Clintons' first term the IRS commissioner was Margaret Milner Richardson, a friend of Hillary's.[4]

Could it be coincidence? "Yes," Grover Norquist, conservative activist and head of Americans for Tax Reform, told the *Times*, "but it's also possible that you could toss a penny in the air a hundred times and have it land heads every time."[5] In March 2000, a bipartisan congressional Joint Taxation Committee investigation disclosed that IRS employees twice reported to U.S. Treasury investigators that the Clinton administration had improperly queried them about sensitive tax information. Staffers in Vice President Al Gore's office sought "the status of certain forms filed by members of a tax-exempt organization." The committee concluded: "These types of contacts lend credence to the allegations that the administration does intervene in IRS matters pertaining to specific taxpayers. The fact that these contacts occurred could raise issues concerning the integrity of the system."[6]

I had my own brush with the law during the Clintons' second administration, when associates of mine at the *American Spectator* were dragged before a grand jury. I first got wind of the probe while sitting in the green room at C-SPAN before being interviewed by Brian Lamb. Onscreen, Lamb asked the very partisan Democratic congressman John Conyers about me and the years of exposés that the *Spectator* had published on the Clintons. "We're investigating the magazine," Conyers unctuously volunteered, whereupon he trotted out his own primitive version of the "Vast Right-Wing Conspiracy." His simpleminded attempt to criminalize the First Amendment amused me, and I was even more amused when he ducked out a side door to avoid greeting me in the hallways as I entered the studio for my interview. The day was, suitably enough, April Fool's Day, 1998.

Less amusing was a letter Deputy Attorney General Eric Holder sent eight days later to independent counsel Ken Starr, calling on him to investigate whether one of his witnesses (and one of my journalistic sources) had been paid off by the magazine to change his testimony. That would be witness tampering, a felony. Holder also claimed we threatened violence against a private citizen. If Starr felt that he had a "conflict of interest," Holder's Justice Department was willing to investigate. The mainstream press recognized the charges as nonsense and paid almost no attention. What resulted was a long and expensive ordeal, a federal investigation that began in June 1998 and lasted fourteen months. A dozen of us were either called in with our lawyers before a Fort Smith, Arkansas, grand jury or before a government inquiry in Washington. Frankly, I found the experience not unrewarding. I had always said the evil of Bill Clinton was not so much his dancing libido but the Clintons' willingness to abuse power. With their attempt to prosecute us I found my claims against them once again vindicated.

Yet the ordeal almost bankrupted the *American Spectator*, badly hurt some utterly blameless citizens, and further coarsened American political life, to say nothing of weakening the First Amendment. With almost no other news sources other than the *Wall Street Journal* and the *Washington Times* objecting, the precedent had been set to harass writers and publications that print unfavorable news about government. In the end, principled people in the Justice Department called in to investigate our case released the judgment that "no prosecution be brought" against us because "many of the allegations, suggestions, and insinuations regarding the tendering and receipt of things of value were shown to be unsubstantiated or, in some cases, untrue." Yet the practice of criminally investigating opposition journalists has now been established—at least for aggrieved Democrats.

The next Clinton administration could benefit from that apparently perfectly acceptable practice. The American press and its First Amendment swamis have yet to object. Could the IRS be politicized again? In the aftermath of the Clintons' wanton use of the IRS, Congress extensively examined the agency. It is unlikely that it will be used politically for years to come. However the next Clinton administration might have even more powerful weapons available for suppressing political opponents. Why abuse the powers of the IRS when one can abuse the "total information awareness" powers permitted to government under that cluster of laws spawned by the post–September 11 Patriot Act? In the name of combating terror, the government can now wiretap; sift through all manner of personal information, from credit card information to library check-outs to phone logs; and all without informing the target of the investigation. In normal times, government investigative powers tend to expand. A Department of

Justice report to the House Judiciary Committee confirmed that such anti-terrorism powers have been used against suspects in crimes other than terrorism, including drug violations and credit card fraud.[7] In abnormal times, when those leading the government have the inclination to suborn institutions and undermine the rule of law, there is no telling how useful these powers could become against political enemies.

"Could you define terrorism as people who stand in front of abortion clinics?" Norquist asks. "Or how about 'hate speech'?" Norquist worries about the legalization of the powers to spy on religious services—both for its effect on moderate Muslims and on how it could be misused in a Clinton administration against conservative Christians.

He adds, with characteristic bluntness, "You can be sure Mrs. Clinton is going to be more interested in what Jerry Falwell says than a sheik."

The Patriot Act and its related laws have been useful instruments when properly used. In the wrong hands, they can become the Alien and Sedition Laws of the twenty-first century, allowing an American president to treat criticism as a crime.

Worst of all, such an approach will be perfectly legal.

CHAPTER EIGHT

How to Defeat Hillary

"Never go outside the experience of your people. When an action or tactic is outside the experience of the people, the result is confusion, fear, and retreat.... Wherever possible go outside of the experience of the enemy."[1]

—*Saul Alinsky*

HILLARY RODHAM CLINTON IS DETERMINED to run for president. Barring the unforeseen, the only barrier between her and the White House is a good Republican campaign. If the Republicans fail and Hillary is elected, she will work through the night like a busy little beaver gnawing away at the rule of law.

Hillary is mendacious and grasping, philosophically and personally corrupt, emblematic of the Coat and Tie Radicals of her generation. Ultimately, she will have it out with the other great ideological sector of the 1960s generation, the penny-loafer conservatives, represented at the moment by President George W. Bush, who stand for normalcy, common sense, and tradition. But it is important to observe one thing. The Republic survived William Jefferson Clinton, and even prospered economically. Though, of course, the Boy President left the country

militarily degraded and diplomatically trivial—with calamitous conse-
quences. Moreover, he intensified the suffocating vapors of the *Kultursmog* so that the country's national conversation as we stepped onto
the bridge to the twenty-first century dwelt on the virtues of boxers vs.
briefs, thongs vs. ladylike discretion, and the need to remove stains from
blue dresses for the protection of presidential immunity.

We can trust that the Republic would also survive Hillary, because
if she were elected the forces of opposition would surge. She would be
boxed in and watched as no president before her. Certainly the *American Spectator* would be watching.

It is fashionable of late to bemoan the role of "hatred" in American politics, at least when that alleged hatred comes from the right.
Leftists now routinely confess their hatred of President George W.
Bush; this is seen as a purely reasonable reaction to the fact that he is
from Texas, apparently believes in the Bible, and sends troops abroad
without the approval of the French and the United Nations. (Witness
a bumper sticker favored by some Democrats: "I am more afraid of
Bush than Saddam.")

I have to wonder, is "hatred" really a problem in American life?
There is a lot to applaud in the high spirits of recent politics. Political
consultants and pollsters are telling their clients that the "base" of both
parties is more partisan, more animated, and more determined to win
than ever before. They report that in the next election, the margin of
victory might no longer be who can mine more votes from the middle third of the electorate that is independent. Victory might go
instead to the party that can do the best job of whipping up its supporters and getting out its base vote.

We have entered into an age of intense partisanship, a cycle that
comes around every other generation in American politics. This is no

contest between football teams. It is a generational contest between competing ideological visions based on differing worldviews. One side or the other will get the upper hand.

At the same time, this generation is not drawing the battle lines of the next American Civil War. I heartily agree that it is no good to be a hater, but I also do not see much hatred among my fellow conservatives, whose disagreements with the Democrats are over political substance and over the importance of high crimes and misdemeanors in high office. Allow me to be gentlemanly enough to aver that there are things to admire and even to like about the Clintons. About Hillary, one cannot help but admire her makeover and new hairdo. She has lost weight. The round face is more angular and somehow softer. The thick eyebrows, which once would have collected coal dust in a Welsh mining village, are well plucked and shaped into pleasant curves. Strangest of all are her eyes. Hillary has actually changed their color. Once they were hazel. Now they are baby blue. "She started experimenting with different blazing blue colors at the White House," a Clinton insider told Matt Drudge. "She even tried turquoise contact lenses once, but it was not a great look for her."[2] Hillary may be a surface phony, but one must acknowledge and even admire her strength, the indefatigable will at her core. In short, I have friends who support the Clintons. I have survived cocktails and even meals with them. I wish such people the very best in every aspect of human existence except electoral success and political influence.

This is the moral way to approach politics. Hatred—true, raw hatred—is an acid on the soul. It is also a loser. We should leave that to the Democrats and their conspiracy theories. I shall take the high road.

Stan Greenberg, a Democratic pollster, found that Hillary's approval ratings shot up about nine points after the rhetorical attacks on her at the Republican national convention in 1992.[3] Call it the Hillary effect. American voters of both sexes are not so used to women in high office that we treat them the way we would treat a man who acts like a victim. So Hillary can have it both ways. She can swell her sails with the desire of millions of Americans, men as well as women, who want to prove that a woman can make it to the top. But in a heartbeat she can turn into the victim, the little lady under assault from a brutal opponent.

This is how Hillary beat Rick Lazio in the 2000 Senate race. At one point in the race, she was accused of once having used an anti-Semitic slur twenty-six years before. The old Hillary would have taken the bait and waded into the story. The new Hillary was wise enough to ignore it. "She didn't react to things," one Republican political consultant says. "She learned how to jujitsu weaknesses into strengths."

She was even cleverer when she faced her opponent directly. In debate, Lazio angrily interrupted Hillary, marched over to her podium, and thrust a piece of paper out for her to sign that would have committed her to a "no soft money" pledge. "Right here, sign it right now!" he shouted. Hillary cringed, and by so doing, soared in the polls. Lazio made a strategic mistake that was even worse. He predicated his whole race on the premise of "stop Hillary." Hillary ran on a platform of seven words: jobs, education, health, Social Security, environment, and choice. Hillary beat Lazio by twelve points.

"One of the odd advantages I had was that everyone already thought they knew everything about me, good or bad," Hillary wrote. "Lazio's attacks were old news. My campaign ignored the personal tone of Lazio's campaign and lasered in on his voting record, as well as his work in Congress as one of Gingrich's top lieutenants."[4]

One leading Republican pollster notes that conservatives tend to dislike Hillary more than Bill—an astonishing level of discontent if you think about it. He adds, "My biggest concern is that Republicans will be so personal and so vitriolic that we actually create sympathy for her."

Hatred is not only bad for the soul. It also clouds judgment and causes one to waste a campaign throwing useless haymakers.

It is important to record Hillary's life record and share it with the receptive public. But that will not be enough to beat Hillary Rodham Clinton when she runs for reelection in 2006, or for the White House. The voters always hold Republicans to a higher standard, because Republicans proclaim themselves to be the party of higher standards. So it will not be good enough to beat Hillary because she deserves to lose.

Her opponent will have to deserve to win.

The first task in deserving to win is to stand resolutely for the main principles of the party. If the GOP is not the party of cutting taxes and smaller government (the latter is, admittedly, a nut that seems never to get cracked), a strong national defense, and a stand for life against abortion, eugenics, and euthanasia, it is nothing. Take away the tax-cutting and smaller government planks, and Republicans lose. Take away the strong national defense plank, and Republicans lose—not only the election, but lives. Take away the protection of life plank, and Republicans lose—not only the election, but the soul of their party.

And of course, the message has to be delivered by someone who believes it, and who is attractive. Lady Thatcher told me at a rather low moment in my ordeal before the Clinton grand jury, "If you have nothing else you have your principles." Sound principles win out in the end. George W. Bush would appear to be a man who in 2004 believes in the soundest of principles, and, luckily, the party has no shortage of such candidates for 2008. The penny-loafer conservatives of the 1960s generation have been toughened by the struggles of recent decades and by the bigotry of the *Kultursmog*. Those following them have learned their lessons.

Beyond that, however, the issue will inevitably be Hillary. So here's a six-point program for how a Republican could put forward a winning platform against Hillary after securing the Republican base:

First, remind the voters of Hillarycare—her failed attempt to socialize 14 percent of the economy, make all of our doctors government employees, and reduce our level of health care to that of Canada's, where people grow old before they get to the front of the line to have their tonsils out, or England's, where dental care apparently is a luxury.

Secondly, Hillary was co-president, so Bill's record is legitimately also hers for criticism. Let her explain the wisdom of the Boy President's impetuous, frenetic, and pointless military deployments and retreats around the world. Why were we sailing around the blue waters of Haiti rather than responding vigorously to terrorist attacks on Americans abroad? Why did we leave Osama bin Laden free rein of the deserts of the Sudan and Afghanistan, though he had publicly declared war against us? Why did the Clinton administration slash the military budget to the point that soldiers' families had to go on food stamps? Past issues of the *American Spectator* should be thoroughly scoured for innumerable other examples.

Third, Hillary is a lawyer, she rakes in huge contributions from trial lawyers, and believes in an activist judiciary. Put her on the spot about the sorry state of civil justice in a lawsuit-crazy country. Make her defend judicial activism. There is never any shortage of examples of judges inventing law and making arbitrary decisions from the bench, overturning democratically enacted legislation and democratically approved initiatives. Make her defend judicial arrogance and the rule of lawyers, and let the Republican candidate stand for strict interpretation of the Constitution, common sense, and the right of the people to govern their own affairs.

Fourth, Hillary, like most leftists, sees international institutions as another means—like the courts—of overruling red-state America. The Republican candidate should keep an eye out for instances of this, if Senator Hillary betrays a belief that military action is morally legit-imate only if the French agree.

Fifth, because of her base and because of her true-believer deafness to the quieter conversations in America, Hillary will almost certainly overreach on the abortion issue. All a Republican has to do is wait for her attack that he would deny a woman's "choice" to say, "With all due respect, Senator Clinton, when a majority of American women take a look at a sonogram, they'll tell you—that's a child, not a choice."

Sixth, contrast Hillary's vision of an America remade by government programs, bureaucrats, judges, and lawyers with a vision of an America sustained by families, communities, and houses of worship. The American vision has always been one of freedom. Freedom is expressly contrary to Hillary's vision, the vision of the Coat and Tie Radical who sees us all in need for "remolding society," which is a polite way of saying that what you and I really need is more social control in our lives. Freedom is, nevertheless, the vision of most

Americans, from the penny-loafer conservative to the small business-man to the church bake sale volunteer. Freedom is the word. Freedom is the cause. And we need to show that if Madame Hillary loses, freedom wins.

Acknowledgments

"Infirm of purpose! Give me the daggers."

So speaks Shakespeare's Lady Macbeth to her blubbering husband after he suffers an uncharacteristic spasm of conscience. Today, after over two decades of being a power behind Bill Clinton's throne, our own Lady Macbeth, Hillary Rodham Clinton, has grasped the daggers and set out to capture a throne of her own.

All this I relate in the slender book you hold in your hands. It was a pleasure to write, and I want to acknowledge some of the many who assisted me in the endeavor. Foremost is Mark Davis, who is a pleasure to work with. His knowledge of Hillary is vast and perceptive, but more impressive still is his knowledge of American politics, particularly as practiced in our nation's capital. Al Regnery, who while the president of Regnery Publishing oversaw publication of two bestsellers for me, has left that fabled publishing house where his family name hangs on the door and become my colleague at *The American Spectator,* where he serves as the best publisher I have ever worked with. Cool, intelligent, witty, and tireless, he is the finest acquisition since Jackie snagged Aristotle Onassis. His advice in writing this book has been invaluable, as has the advice of my editor Harry Crocker, as fine an editor as he is a writer. My colleague through battles won and lost, Executive Editor of *The American Spectator,* Wlady Pleszczynski, is always a help in every literary effort and a human database for which I am grateful. My wife, Jeanne, a useful critic and cheerful companion, developed into a splendid photographer while I wrote, as well as an accomplished student of abnormal psychology. Much love Jeanne.

Finally, I would like to acknowledge my debt to Robert L. Bartley, Editor Emeritus of the *Wall Street Journal,* who upon retiring as the most influential editorial page editor in the country became Senior Editorial Adviser to *The American Spectator.* For the last three years of his life he advised me on a wide range of subjects from economics, to politics, to the Byzantine world of the Clintons, and on to happier matters, such as the perfect martini and the technical fluency of his new Jaguar—resplendent in British Racing Green. In the last two years of his life he held off a raging cancer without melodrama but with the quiet resolve in which he had always led his life, the life of one of the most interesting minds I have ever encountered. He was the loyalest of friends, and to the best of my ability I shall carry on his work.

—R. Emmett Tyrrell, Jr.
Alexandria, Virginia
December 12, 2003

I am very grateful to Rebecca, who undertook the logistics of not one, but two, moves and endless soccer games while I was spending my time working the phones and the computer. This work is also made possible by the many people in politics, Democrats as well as Republicans, who trusted us with their close-in view of the workings of the U.S. Senate.

—Mark W. Davis

Notes

INTRODUCTION

1. Carl Limbacher, et al., "'GI Bill' Following 'Marine' Hillary's Example," NewsMax.com, August 2, 2002.

2. Two members who did surface in the press were Jack Palladino and Terry Lenzner.

CHAPTER ONE: DRIVING THE PARTY

1. Saul Alinsky, *Rules for Radicals: A Practical Primer for Realistic Radicals* (New York: Random House, 1971), 149.

2. Lorraine Woellert, "The Evolution of Campaign Finance?" *BusinessWeek*, September 15, 2003.

3. Richard Reeves, *Hartford Courant*, August 27, 2003.

4. Jim Dwyer, "Senator Clinton Says No to '04, but Playfulness Hints at Yes," *New York Times,* September 9, 2003.

5. Ibid.

6. Dierdre Shesgreen, "Forget the 10 Democrats Running; Hillary Clinton Draws the Most Buzz," *St. Louis Post-Dispatch*, September 25, 2003.

7. Raymond Hernandez, "A Wary Mrs. Clinton Runs a Perpetual Race," *New York Times*, October 18, 2003.

8. Deborah Orin and Vincent Morris, "Hillary Hoards PAC $$," *New York Post*, September 8, 2003.

9. Deborah Orin, "Charity Begins at Home for Hill's Pol Fund," *New York Post,* September 8, 2003.

10. Woellert, "The Evolution of Campaign Finance?"

11. Jim VandeHei, "Clinton Develops Into a Force in the Senate Growing Role in Policy, Fundraising Fuels Talk of '08 Campaign," *Washington Post*, March 5, 2003.

12. Hillary Clinton, *Living History* (New York: Simon & Schuster, 2003), 423.

13. Alexander Bolton, "It's Hard to Be Humble When You're Hillary," *The Hill*, March 25, 2003.

14. David Maraniss, *First in His Class* (New York: Touchstone Books, 1996), 326.

CHAPTER TWO: THE DAY JOB

1. Saul Alinsky, *Rules for Radicals: A Practical Primer for Realistic Radicals* (New York: Random House, 1971), 59.

2. Hillary Clinton, *Living History* (New York: Simon & Schuster, 2003), 374.

3. Connie Bruck, "Hillary the Pol," *New Yorker*, May 30, 1994.

4. Michelle Malkin, Townhall.com, September 16, 2001.

5. Michael Kelly, "Blame Hillary," *Jewish World Review*, July 15, 1999.

6. Ibid., "New Hope for Nice Guys," August 3, 2000.

7. Alexander Bolton, "Workhorse or Senatorial Stalking Horse?" *The Hill*, March 26, 2003.

8. Clinton, 434.

9. Press release, April 17, 2003.

10. Gail Russell Chaddock, "Clinton's Quiet Path to Power," *Christian Science Monitor*, April 28, 2003.

11. Ibid.

12. Guy Coates, "Challenge in Last Senate Race of 2002," Associated Press, December 8, 2002.

13. Robert Novak, "Helping Hillary," Townhall.com, January 18, 2003.

14. Jim VandeHei, "Clinton Develops Into a Force in the Senate Growing Role in Policy, Fundraising Fuels Talk of '08 Campaign," *Washington Post*, March 5, 2003.

15. Sheryl Gay Stolberg, "With Democrats Divided on War, Pelosi Faces First Test," *New York Times*, March 31, 2003.

16. "Aid & Comfort," *New York Post*, March 19, 2003.

17. Deborah Orin, "Even Dems Say It Was 'Compelling,'" *New York Post*, February 6, 2003.

18. Ibid., "Hill Sort of Backs W.," March 5, 2003.

19. Andrew Sullivan, "Hillary's Military Campaign for the Presidency," *Sunday Times,* May 11, 2003.

20. Stephen Dinan, "Hillary says 'No' but acts like a candidate," *Washington Times*, September 25, 2003.

21. William Kristol, "The War for Liberalism," *Weekly Standard*, April 7, 2003.

22. Alinsky, 28.

23. Ibid., 78.

24. Todd Connor and Carl Cameron, FOX News Channel, August 30, 2003.

25. Deborah Orin, "Dim Dems Playing Body-Bag Politics," *New York Post*, January 30, 2003.

26. Bobby Eberle, "GOPUSA," *Talon News*, July 30, 2003.

27. Vincent Morris, "Hillary Joins War Over Judge Pick," *New York Post*, February 12, 2003.

28. Richard Roeper, "Even American Heroes Capable of Being Jerks," *Chicago Sun-Times*, October 25, 2001.

CHAPTER THREE: LIVID HISTORY

1. Hillary Clinton, *It Takes a Village* (New York: Simon & Schuster, 1996), 147.

2. "Writer's Block Snags Clintons," *New York Post*, April 8, 2003.

3. Yahoo News, April 28, 2003.

4. David Kirkpatrick, "Author Clinton Shakes Many Hands and Sells Many Books," *New York Times*, July 26, 2003.

5. "People in the News," Associated Press, July 7, 2003.

6. Henry Louis Gates, Jr., "Hating Hillary," *New Yorker*, February 26, 1996.

7. Richard Lacayo, "The Ghost and Mrs. Clinton," *Time*, January 22, 1996.

8. Hillary Clinton, *Living History* (New York: Simon & Schuster, 2003), 529.

9. Ibid., 311.

10. Interview with the author, June 13, 2003.

11. Clinton, *Living History*, 428.

12. CNN.com, June 9, 2003.

13. Clinton, *Living History*, 95.

14. Ambrose Evans-Pritchard, *The Secret Life of Bill Clinton* (Washington, D.C.: Regnery, 1997), 241–242.

15. Pat Griffith, "Group Urges Panel To Expand Queries," *Pittsburgh Post-Gazette*, September 29, 1998.

16. Barbara Olson, *Hell to Pay* (Washington, D.C.: Regnery, 1999), 273.

17. Jerry Zeifman, "Hillary's Watergate Scandal," *New York Post*, August 16, 1999.

18. Jerry Zeifman, *Without Honor: the Impeachment of President Nixon and The Crimes of Camelot* (New York: Thunder's Mouth Press, 1995), 123.

19. Ibid., 155.

20. Clinton, *Living History*, 465–466.

21. Ibid., 441.

22. Sidney Blumenthal, *The Clinton Wars* (New York: Farrar Straus & Giroux, 2003), 465.

23. *American Spectator*, August, 1996.

24. David Maraniss, *First in His Class* (New York: Touchstone Books, 1996), 327.

25. Ibid., 320.

26. Ibid., 321.

27. Ibid., 441.

28. Ibid., 450.

29. Clinton, *Living History*, 441.

30. Joe Conason, *The Hunting of the President* (New York: St. Martin's Press, 2000), 113.

31. David Brock, "Living with the Clintons," *American Spectator*, January 1994.

32. Michael Kelly, "Blame Hillary," *Jewish World Review*, July 15, 1999.

33. Clinton, *Living History*, 194.

34. Neely Tucker and Susan Schmidt, "Lewinsky Case Report Released; Prosecutors Could Have Indicted Clinton, Ray Says," *Washington Post*, March 7, 2002.

35. Robert L. Bartley, "No Wars, Only Scandals," *Wall Street Journal*, May 28, 2003.

36. Jackie Bennett, Timothy Susanin, and Solomon Wisenberg, "Starr Wars Revisited," *Washington Post*, July 5, 2003.

37. Carol D. Leonnig, "Clintons Lose Legal Fees Claim," *Washington Post*, July 16, 2003.

38. Clinton, *Living History*, 86.

39. Ibid., 87.

40. Olson, 141–142.

41. Ibid., 142.

42. Ibid., 143.

43. Clinton, *Living History*, 173.

44. Neil A. Lewis, "New Criticism of First Lady In Final Travel Office Report," *New York Times*, October 19, 2000.

45. FOX News Channel, "Hannity & Colmes," June 10, 2003.

46. "Clinton Corruption Plays Us for Fools—We Won't Forget," *New York Observer*, March 5, 2001.

CHAPTER FOUR: AN IDEOLOGICAL LIFE

1. "Hillary's New Low," *American Prowler*, March 31, 2003.

2. Interview with the author.

3. "Washington Whispers," *U.S. News & World Report*, April 7, 2003.

4. Steven F. Hayward, "Old Liberalism, R.I.P.," *National Review Online*, March 27, 2003.

5. Daniel Patrick Moynihan, December 10, 1997.

6. Daniel Patrick Moynihan and Suzanne Weaver, *A Dangerous Place* (Boston: Little, Brown, 1978), 8.

7. We are indebted here to the analysis of Steven F. Hayward. For a more comprehensive look at Moynihan's place in modern politics, turn to Hayward's *The Age of Reagan: The Fall of the Old Liberal Order, 1964–1980*.

8. Hayward, "Old Liberalism, R.I.P."

9. Saul Alinsky, *Rules for Radicals: A Practical Primer for Realistic Radicals* (New York: Random House, 1971), 79.

10. Hillary Clinton, *Living History* (New York: Simon & Schuster, 2003), Appendix.

11. Alinsky, 30.

12. Ibid., 130.

13. Ibid., 21–22.

14. Barbara Olson, *Hell to Pay* (Washington, D.C.: Regnery, 1999), 312.

15. Michael Kelly, "Saint Hillary," *New York Times Magazine,* May 23, 1993.

16. Interview with the author.

17. Daniel Wattenberg, "Love and Hate in Arkansas," *American Spectator,* April/May 1994; David Brock, "Living with the Clintons," *American Spectator,* January 1994.

18. Hillary Clinton, Wellesley Commencement Address, May 31, 1969.

19. Alinsky, 51.

20. Ibid., 11.

21. Ibid., 13.

22. Ibid., 33.

23. Ibid., 24–25.

24. Ibid., 25.

25. Ibid., xvii.

26. Clinton, *Living History,* 38.

27. Alinsky, xxiii.

28. Actually, if Hillary had been at the Grant Park demonstrations, she might have been standing near me and my younger brother, all three of us being native Chicagoans. My brother and I were there out of curiosity. On a radio show in New York in the 1990s with Tom Hayden, one of the leaders of the protest at the Democratic convention, I reminded him and our radio audience of why the police finally attacked the demonstrators. In Chicago, my brother and I were on the demonstrators' side of the police line, a foot or two from the young cops, who looked straight ahead, silent and well disciplined. Many of the cops were young Irish-Americans, Italian-Americans, and other working-class ethnics. Hayden and his strategists had counseled their student

protesters to shout into the cops' faces, "Hey, who's at home fucking your wife?" and similar incendiaries. My brother, a football player who had played high school ball with several of the cops nearby, suggested we depart before the cops took action . . . or before he did. We left before the melee, but as I told a subdued Hayden on that radio show, his demonstrators got just the confrontation they sought. They were not disciples of Mahatma Gandhi.

29. Alinsky, xxiii.

30. Clinton, *Living History*, 14.

31. Hillary Clinton, *It Takes a Village* (New York: Simon & Schuster, 1996), 206.

32. Clinton, *Living History*, 36.

33. Clinton, *It Takes a Village*, 22.

34. Ibid., 171.

35. Kelly, "Saint Hillary."

36. Kenneth L. Woodward, "Soulful Matters," *Newsweek*, October 31, 1994.

37. Clinton, *Living History*, 46.

38. Olson, 59.

39. David Maraniss, *First in His Class* (New York: Touchstone Books, 1996), 249.

40. Olson, 62.

41. Clinton, *Living History*, 52.

42. Craig is another of Hillary's comrades who reappeared with her decades later to defend the president against impeachment and to return Elian Gonzalez to Cuba. He will doubtless have a role, along with all the other 1960s lefties we have reintroduced in these pages, in the eventual intergenerational battle with George W. Bush's 1960s conservatives.

43. Maraniss, 262.

44. Meredith Oakley, *On the Make* (Washington, D.C.: Regnery, 1996), 104.

45. Ibid., 106.

46. Clinton, *Living History*, 51–52.

47. Olson, 110.

48. Maraniss, 308.

49. Clinton, *Living History*, 67.

CHAPTER FIVE: THE COMING CAMPAIGN

1. David Maraniss, *First in His Class* (New York: Touchstone Books, 1996), 396.

2. Barbara Olson, *Hell to Pay* (Washington, D.C.: Regnery, 1999), 224.

3. Hillary Clinton, *Living History* (New York: Simon & Schuster, 2003), 510–511.

4. Ibid., 502.

5. Saul Alinsky, *Rules for Radicals: A Practical Primer for Realistic Radicals* (New York: Random House, 1971), 185–186.

6. Ibid., 187.

7. Ibid., 194–195.

8. Hillary Clinton, Senate floor statement, January 9, 2003.

9. Ibid., February 15, 2003.

10. Hillary Clinton, speech to the American Society of Newspaper Editors, April 5, 2001.

11. Grant Schulte, "Pro-life women shift to majority; Most want abortion to be prohibited or limited, poll says," *Washington Times*, July 2, 2003.

12. Clinton, *Living History*, 417–418.

13. Ibid., 381.

14. *American Prowler,* December 1, 2003

15. *Sydney Morning Herald,* November 27, 2003

16. Hillary Clinton, address to John Jay College, January 24, 2003.

17. Clinton, *Living History*, 357.

18. Carl Lindbacher, et al., "Bill Got Facts Wrong on Bin Laden Confession," Newsmax.com, August 6, 2003.

19. Clinton, *Living History*, 262.

20. Interview with the author.

21. Connie Bruck, "Hillary the Pol," *New Yorker*, May 30, 1994.

22. Interview with the author.

23. Alinsky, 136.

CHAPTER SIX: FATAL ATTRACTION

1. Michael Barone, "Hillary 2008," *Wall Street Journal*, June 19, 2003.

2. Susan Estrich, "The Clintons are Back," Creators Syndicate, May 14, 2003.

3. Laura Blumenfeld, "John Kerry: Hunter, Dreamer, Realist," *Washington Post*, June 1, 2003.

4. Sidney Blumenthal, *The Clinton Wars* (New York: Farrar Straus & Giroux, 2003), 794.

5. Michael Barone, *The Almanac of American Politics 1994* (Washington, D.C.: National Journal Group, 1994), xxxi.

6. Ibid., xxiv.

7. Michael Wines, "The Health Care Debate," *New York Times*, July 25, 1994.

8. Michelle Cottle, "The Wrong Race," *New Republic*, June 7, 1999.

9. Estrich, "The Clintons are Back."

CHAPTER SEVEN: THE PRESIDENCY OF CLINTON 44

1. Saul Alinsky, *Rules for Radicals: A Practical Primer for Realistic Radicals* (New York: Random House, 1971), 34.

2. Interview with the author.

3. Hillary Clinton, *Living History* (New York: Simon & Schuster, 2003), 237–238.

4. Jerry Seper and Bill Sammon, "IRS audits of conservatives get a close look," *Washington Times*, September 29, 1997.

5. Ibid.

6. Associated Press, "The White House Tried to Get Taxpayer Data," *Washington Times*, March 16, 2000.

7. Dan Eggen, "Anti-Terror Power Used Broadly; Laws Invoked Against Crimes Unrelated to Terror, Report Says," *Washington Post*, May 21, 2003.

CHAPTER EIGHT: HOW TO DEFEAT HILLARY

1. Saul Alinsky, *Rules for Radicals: A Practical Primer for Realistic Radicals* (New York: Random House, 1971), 127–128.

2. Drudge Report, June 25, 2003.

3. Margaret Carlson, "All Eyes on Hillary," *Time*, September 14, 1992.

4. Hillary Clinton, *Living History* (New York, Simon & Schuster, 2003), 519.

Index

ABA. *See* American Bar Association
ABC, 75
abortion, 130, 144–46
Adams, Abigail, 191
adultery, 4
Afghanistan, 46, 206
AFL-CIO, 27
Africa, 154
African-Americans: Clinton and, 21; Landrieu's alienation of, 5, 41–42
Agnew, Spiro, 114, 162
Albright, Madeleine, 153
Alien and Sedition Laws, 200
Alinsky, Saul, 35, 47, 51, 128, 159; amoral cynicism of, 121; career of, 115–16; classes in society and, 116–17; Democratic Party and, 121; Hillary's ideology and, 101, 105–8, 112–20; middle class and, 141; power and, 7, 126; rules of politics and, 106–8; truth and, 105
All Too Human (Stephanopoulos), 82
Allen, Bill, 158
Allen, George, 157–58
Ambrose, Stephen, 134–35
America Votes, 27, 33
American Bar Association (ABA), 30
American Constitution Society for Law and Policy, 29, 30
American Federation of State, County, and Municipal Employees, 27
American President, The, 134
American Society of Newspaper Editors, 143–44

American Spectator, 80, 83, 85, 150, 170, 202, 206; Clintons' misuse of IRS and, 197–99
Americans Coming Together, 27, 33
Americans for Tax Reform, 197
Amin, Idi, 102
Angola, 193
AnShell Media, 31, 33
Arafat, Suha, 50, 152
Arkansas, 2, 8, 17, 73, 111
Armed Services Committee, 15, 42, 46–50
arms control test bans, 47
Arvad, Inga, 169
Aspin, Les, 178–79
AT&T, 140
Atwater, Lee, 108

Baez, Joan, 193
Baker, Peter, 81
Balderston, Kris, 195
Barnett, Bob, 80, 81
Barone, Michael, 179–80
Bayh, Evan, 194
Begala, Paul, 189
Begley, Ed, Jr., 9
Behind the Oval Office: Getting Reelected Against All Odds (Morris), 112
Bennett, Mickey, 14
Berger, Debbie, 28
Berger, Samuel, 28
Berlin, Germany, 68
Biden, Joseph, 145
Bilbo, Theodore, 56

bin Laden, Osama, 31, 86, 153–54, 206
Black Panthers, 3, 30, 124, 125, 126
Blair, Jim, 90
Blair, Tony and Cherie, 71
Bloodworth-Thomason, Linda, 188
Blumenthal, Sidney, 81, 169, 170, 173
Blumstein, James, 125
Boeing, 140
Bone, Robert "Red", 90
Bosnia, 80
Boston, Mass., 19, 20
Boy Clinton. *See* Clinton, William Jefferson
Boy Clinton (Tyrrell), 85
Breach, The (Baker), 81
Broaddrick, Juanita, 92–94
Broder, David, 194
Brooke, Edward, 114
Brookings Institute, 29
Brown, Becky, 110
Brown, Kent Masterson, 197
Bryan, William Jennings, 9
Buchanan, Pat, 129
Burns, James McGregor, 165
Bush, Barbara, 190
Bush, George H. W., 32, 175; 1992 presidential campaign and, 8; bin Laden and, 31; Gore vs., 184; Hillary as president and, 190; Iran-Contra affair and, 89; victories of, 177
Bush, George W., 14, 21, 46, 163; abortion and, 144–46; approval ratings of, 12; campaign finance and, 22, 41; conservatism and, 106; Enron and, 26; Hillary's criticism of, 39, 47–48, 52–55, 135–36, 142–43, 151–52; Hillary's presidential ambitions and, 157; Hillary as president and, 188; homeland security and, 53–55, 151–52; Israel and, 153; Left-Behind America and, 140; Operation Iraqi Freedom and, 48–49, 147; penny-loafer conservatives and, 6; September 11 and, 37, 52, 53; Soros and, 27; tax cuts and, 26, 142–43, 152

Bush, Jeb, 158
Bush, Laura, 188
BusinessWeek, 9, 27
Byrd, Robert C., 39, 56

Calhoun, John C., 100
California, 9, 10, 48, 148
campaign finance: Democratic Party and, 6, 22–29; Hollywood and, 22; labor unions and, 22; McCain-Feingold law and, 9, 22, 26, 59–60; Republican Party and, 22–23
Capitalism and Freedom (Friedman), 106
Capone, Al, 115
Capra, Frank, 56
Carlos the Jackal, 153
Carlyle Group, 31
Carnahan, Mel, 20–21
Caro, Robert, 46
Carter, Jimmy, 20, 166, 177
Carville, James, 81, 184, 189
Castro, Fidel, 123
Cato Institute, 28
cattle futures, 26, 74, 96, 118
Center for American Progress, 28–29, 33
Center for the Advancement of Women, 145
Central Intelligence Agency (CIA), 153, 154, 171
Chafee, Lincoln, 44
Chappaqua, N.Y., 11, 22, 25, 62, 95
Chavez, Cesar, 116
Chechens, 49
Cheney, Dick, 49
Chicago, Ill., 20, 116
Chicago, University of, 115
Chicago Eight, 124
"Children Under the Law" (Clinton), 129
Children's Defense Fund, 128, 147
children's rights, 128–31
China, 49, 146
CIA. *See* Central Intelligence Agency
civil rights, 103

Civil Rights Act (1957), 56
Civil Rights Act (1964), 56
Claremont McKenna College, 138
Clark, Wesley, 5, 11, 13–15, 17–18, 194
Clay, Henry, 100
Clinton, Chelsea, 70, 71, 90
Clinton, Hillary Rodham: 2006 Senate reelection of, 13, 17, 62–65; appearance of, 2; in Arkansas, 2–4, 17; Armed Services Committee and, 46–50; as author, 29, 39, 67–97, 122; campaign finance and, 6, 9, 11, 22–29; cattle futures and, 26, 74, 118; as co-president, 7, 86–94, 154–55; defeating, 201–8; Democratic Party and, 4–6, 7–34, 45–46, 161–85; election 2004 and, 9–21; election 2008 and, 59; feminism of, 94; as first lady, 4, 7, 17–18, 37; as governor's wife, 4; health care and, 37, 51, 101; homeland security and, 40, 50–55; ideology of, 99–132; marriage of, 68, 82–86, 156; mystique of, 21–32; as president, 187–200; presidential ambitions of, 1, 7–34, 133–59; radicalism of, 1–4, 51, 94–97, 104–5, 111–12; Republican Party and, 13, 38–39, 44, 51–52; as running mate, 13–18; in Senate, 4, 5, 8, 35–65, 99–106; Steering and Coordination Committee and, 5, 25
Clinton, Roger, 74, 76–77, 95
Clinton, William Jefferson, 11, 175–77; 1992 presidential campaign and, 7–8, 12; African-Americans and, 21; campaign finance and, 6, 9, 11, 22–29; Clark and, 15; Democratic Party and, 4–6, 12, 16, 19, 21, 23–29, 161–85; draft evasion of, 2; Hillary's presidential ambitions and, 9, 12, 16, 18, 19, 33–34, 155–57; Hollywood and, 9–10; impeachment of, 25, 60, 79, 131–32; Lewinsky scandal and, 74, 79; marriage of, 68, 82–86, 156; mystique of, 21–24; pardons of, 95;

sex scandals and, 80–86, 92–94, 110; Whitewater and, 25, 58
Clinton Wars, The (Blumenthal), 81, 169
cloning, 144
CNN, 155
Coat and Tie Radicals: Alinsky's amorality and, 117; children's rights and, 129; Clinton administration and, 125; Democratic Party and, 121; freedom in society and, 207; Hillary and, 1, 4, 6, 48, 74, 128; penny-loafer conservatives vs., 6, 106–15
Cohen, William, 194
Cold War, 103, 177
Cole, Johnetta, 193
Collins, Susan, 44
Columbia University, 57
Communist Party, 30
Conscience of a Conservative (Goldwater), 120
conservatism: Hillary's hatred of, 44; media and, 32; paranoid style and, 75; penny-loafer, 6, 106–15; Republican Party and, 29
Constitution, 4, 137, 146
Cook, Charlie, 40
Coolidge, Calvin, 121
Cornyn, John, 56
Corzine, Jon, 31
Couric, Katie, 39, 67–68
Craig, Greg, 127–28
Craig, Larry, 41
Craighead, Kelly, 195–96
Crane, Dan, 176
Critical Legal Studies (Crits), 126, 128
Crits. See Critical Legal Studies
C-SPAN, 198
Cuomo, Andrew, 5

D'Amato, Al, 60
Daily Star, 40
Dal Col, Bill, 139, 157
Dale, Billy, 197
Daley, Richard J., 121

Daley, Richard M., 195
A Dangerous Place (Moynihan), 103, 104
Daschle, Tom, 23, 31, 40, 44–46, 48, 145
Davis, Angela, 30
Davis, Gray, 10, 64, 163
Davis, Mark W., 6
Dean, Howard: attack on, 137; Clintons and Democratic Party and, 162, 164; Hillary's presidential ambitions and, 5, 11, 15–16, 19, 126; Hollywood donor base and, 9
Decter, Midge, 104
defense. *See* homeland security
Defense Authorization Bill, 149
DeLay, Tom, 23, 39, 175
Dellinger, Walter, 29
Democratic Leadership Council, 29, 147
Democratic National Committee (DNC), 5, 25, 27
Democratic Party: Alinsky and, 121; campaign finance and, 6, 22–29; change in, 121; Clintons and, 4, 7–34, 161–85; collapse of, 13, 19–20; education and, 26; health care and, 26; Hillary and, 7–34; homeland security and, 54; infrastructure of, 6; internal policy agenda of, 45; judicial nominations and, 55–59; left and, 1, 104; liberalism and, 104; myth and, 164–78; in New York, 5; Republican Party vs., 180–85; Truman wing of, 149
Democratic Policy Committee, 31
Demzilla, 27
Derrida, Jacques, 126
Diallo, Amadou, 63
Dirksen, Everett, 56
DNC. *See* Democratic National Committee
Dole, Bob, 12
Dole, Elizabeth, 36, 158
Donahue, Phil, 30
Dorgan, Byron, 31

Douglas, Michael, 134
DreamWorks SKG, 9
Drobny, Sheldon and Anita, 31
Drudge, Matt, 203
Dublin, Ireland, 73
Dukakis, Michael, 166, 195
Duke, Doris, 85
Duke University, 36
Durbin, Richard, 44

East Hampton, N.Y., 11
Eastman Kodak, 116, 119, 138
Edelman, Marian Wright, 128, 175
The Editors, 16
education, 26, 149
Edwards, John, 13–15
Egypt, 177
Eisenhower, Dwight D., 177
Elders, Joycelyn, 194
election 2004, Hillary's presidential ambitions and, 9–21, 157
election 2008, Hillary's presidential ambitions and, 59, 157–58
Energy, Department of, 53
Engels, Friedrich, 106
Enron, 26
environment, 2, 52–53
Environment and Public Works Committee, 65
Environmental Protection Agency (EPA), 52–53
EPA. *See* Environmental Protection Agency
equality, 2
Esquire, 106
Estrada, Miguel, 57, 58
Estrich, Susan, 163, 185
Exner, Judith, 169

Fabiani, Mark, 14
Fahnestock, Marion "Mimi", 170
Faircloth, Lauch, 13–14
Falwell, Jerry, 200
family, 130–31
FBI. *See* Federal Bureau of Investigation

Federal Bureau of Investigation (FBI), 74, 77, 153
Federalist, 58
Federalist Society, 29–30
Feingold, Russ, 59, 61
Feinman, Barbara, 69–70
Feinstein, Dianne, 24
Ferraro, Geraldine, 17
Filegate, 76, 77
filibustering, 55–59
First in His Class (Maraniss), 33, 83, 127
Fischer, Bobby, 46
Fiske, Robert, 14, 86
Florida, 18, 27, 148
Flowers, Gennifer, 82, 177
Foley, Tom, 179
Forbes, Steve, 139
Ford, Gerald, 20, 103, 121
Fort Drum, N.Y., 46
Fortas, Abe, 56
Foster, Vince, 74, 77–78, 91, 96, 110
Founding Fathers, 122
FOX News Channel, 30–31, 32, 92
Franken, Al, 31
Fray, Mary Lee, 82
Fray, Paul, 82, 83
Friedman, Milton, 106, 144
Friends in High Places (Hubbell), 111
Friends of Hillary, 24, 27, 31
Frist, Bill, 41, 51, 157
fund-raising. *See* campaign finance

Garry, Charles, 124, 125
Geffen, David, 9, 15
Georgia, 47, 48, 49
Gephardt, Richard, 11, 50
Giancana, Sam, 169
Gingrich, Newt, 96, 154, 161, 175, 181, 204
Giuliani, Rudy, 13, 14, 52; crime and, 103; Hillary's 2006 Senate reelection and, 63–65; Hillary's presidential ambitions and, 158
Global Crossing, 26
Goldwater, Barry, 29, 71, 120, 122, 124

Gonzales, Alberto, 58
GOP. *See* Republican Party
Gore, Al, 10, 17, 176, 197; Campaign 2000 and, 167, 184; class welfare and, 147; left and media and, 30–31; performance politics and, 37
Graham, Bob, 15
Granholm, Jennifer, 194
Grant Park, 119, 124
Great Leap Forward, 2
Greenberg, Stan, 148, 203–4
Guinier, Lani, 194

Haiti, 206
Hamilton, Alexander, 58
Hamilton, Lee, 194
Hannity & Colmes, 92–94
Hannity, Sean, 32
Harding, Warren G., 74, 157
Hart, Gary, 83
Harvard Business School, 6
Harvard Educational Review, 129
Harvard Law School, 36, 57
Havana, Cuba, 118
Hayward, Steven F., 104
health care: Clinton and, 51; Democratic Party and, 26; Hillary and, 37; objections to, 101–2; Republican Party and, 13
Heber Springs, Ark., 111
Heidegger, Martin, 106
Hell to Pay (Olson), 1
Helms, Jesse, 14, 44
Heritage Foundation, 28, 196
Hightower, Jim, 30
Hill Raisers, 24
Hill's Angels, 24
HILLPAC, 23–25, 29, 33
Himalayas, 73
Hiss, Alger, 75, 87
Hitler, Adolf, 169
Ho Chi Minh, 123
Hofstadter, Richard, 75
Holder, Eric, 198
Hollings, Ernest, 145

Hollywood, 9–10, 22
homeland security, 47; Bush and, 53–55, 151–52; Democratic Party and, 54; Hillary and, 40, 50–55; myth of, 54; Republican Party and, 13; spending for, 54–55
Homeland Security Block Grant Act, 54
Homeland Security Department, 54
Hoover, Herbert, 189
House Judiciary Impeachment Inquiry, 78, 131
House of Representatives, 180
Hubbell, Webb, 88, 111
Humphrey, Hubert, 121
Hussein, Saddam, 48, 49, 137, 177, 202
Hutchinson, Kay Bailey, 43, 158–59
Hyatt, Joel, 31

Ickes, Harold, 155, 196; Clinton fund-raising and, 11, 26, 27; Hillary's presidential ambitions and, 9
Idaho, 41
Illinois, 44, 46
India, 49, 102
Institute for Policy Studies, 29
Internal Revenue Service (IRS), 196–99
Iowa, 27, 137
Iran, 71
Iran-Contra affair, 89, 178
Iraq, 43, 71
Iraq War. *See* Operation Iraqi Freedom
Islamabad, Pakistan, 73
Israel, 48, 50, 152–53, 177
It Takes a Village (Clinton), 68, 69–70; God and, 122
It's Academic, 133

Jackson, Andrew, 157, 163
Jackson, Henry "Scoop", 149
Jefferson, Thomas, 163
Jiang Qing, 1, 4
Jockey Club, 171, 172
John Birch Society, 75
John Jay College, 151

Johnson, Betsy, 119
Johnson, Lyndon B., 19, 29, 33, 46, 169, 56
Johnson, Norma Holloway, 87
Jones, Don, 121–23, 128
Jones, Julia Hughes, 81–82
Jones, Paula Corbin, 88, 177, 197
judicial nominations, 55–59
Jungle, The (Sinclair), 116
Justice Department, 27, 57, 90, 199, 200

Kantor, Mickey, 125
Katmandu, Nepal, 73
Katzenberg, Jeffrey, 9
Kawior, Philip, 46, 47, 70–71, 157, 164
Kelly, Michael, 37, 86, 109–10, 122
Kemp, Jack, 139
Kendall, David, 81, 87
Kennedy, Bobby, 47
Kennedy, Duncan, 126
Kennedy, Edward, 20
Kennedy, John F., 19, 22, 25, 35, 157, 165, 168–71, 150
Kennedy, Robert F., 20, 119, 124
Kennedy, Ted, 57
Kennedy, William, 77
Kent State, 124, 125
Kerry, John, 11, 15, 19, 137, 164, 167
Kierkegaard, Søren, 2
Kilgore, Ed, 18–19
Kincaid, Diane, 33
King, Martin Luther, Jr., 123
Kirk, Russell, 106
Kirkpatrick, Jeane, 104
Kristol, Irving, 104
Kristol, William, 50
Krock, Arthur, 170
Ku Klux Klan, 56
Kulturkampf, 142
Kultursmog, 71, 97, 105, 124, 131, 163, 165, 167, 169, 172, 181, 194, 202, 206
Kuntsler, William, 125
Kuwait, 177

LaBella, Charles, 27
labor unions, 5, 22, 27–28
Lake Placid, N.Y., 134
Lamb, Brian, 198
Landrieu, Mary, 5, 41–43
Lasater, Dan, 77
Lauer, Matt, 52
Lautenberg, Frank, 20
Lazio, Rick, 139, 148, 204
left: 1960s, 1, 2; America's institutions and, 1; Democratic Party and, 1, 104; Hillary and, 1–4, 104–5; media and, 30–32; Methodism and, 123–24
Left-Behind America, 138–42
Legal Services Corporation, 17
Lenin, Vladimir, 126
Lerner, Michael, 109–11, 113, 118, 122
Lewinsky, Monica, 74, 75, 79, 82, 84, 86, 177
Lewis, John L., 116
liberalism, 104
Lieberman, Joseph, 15, 17
Life magazine, 108, 124
Limbacher, Carl, 154
Limbaugh, Rush, 30, 31, 32, 64, 181
Lincoln, Abraham, 13
Lindsay, John, 124
Lindsey, Bruce, 14
Living History (Clinton), 67–97, 124; abortion and, 146; Alinsky and, 118; Atwater and, 108; book tour for, 39; children's rights and, 131; Clinton's sex scandals and, 80–86; conspiracies and, 75–76; DeLay and, 39; Hillary's claims to innocence and, 88–90; Hillary's dishonesty and, 78–81; Hillary's presidential ambitions and, 148; Hillary as co-president and, 86–94; Hillary as first lady and, 71; Lerner and, 110, 118; problems with, 67, 68–69; public response to, 94–97; publicity for, 67–68; refurbishing the record in, 70–71, 74, 78; Republican Party and, 29, 121; scandals and, 73–78, 91–94; travel and, 72–73
Livingstone, Craig, 77
London, England, 68
Long, Huey, 56
Long Island, N.Y., 11
Los Angeles Times, 83
Losing bin Laden (Miniter), 153
Louisiana, 5, 41, 42
Lowey, Nita, 20
Luzzatto, Tamera, 195

Machiavelli, Niccolo, 116
Madame Hillary. See Clinton, Hillary Rodham
Madison Guaranty, 90
Malkin, Michelle, 37
Mao Zedong, 1, 4
Maoism, 123, 140
Maraniss, David, 33, 83, 127, 131, 133
Marcuse, Herbert, 106, 127, 128
Marist College Institute, 13
marriage, 130–31
Marshall Plan, 177
Marx, Karl, 106, 118
McAuliffe, Terry, 5, 9–10, 16, 25–27
McCain, John, 59
McCain-Feingold law, 9, 22, 26, 59–60
McCarthy, Eugene, 119, 124
McCarthy, Joseph R., 114
McCartney, Paul, 63
McDermott, Jim, 48, 50
McDougal, Susan, 95, 177
McEntee, Gerald, 27
McGovern, George, 50, 104, 134–35, 175
McKinley, William, 84
McKinney, Cynthia, 48, 50
McLarty, Mack, 91
McLean, Va., 94
McVeigh, Timothy, 181
media, 30–32
Medicaid, 135
Medicare, 26, 135, 143
Meet the Press, 49

Methodism, 121–24; left and, 123–24
Michigan, 148
Microsoft, 90
Middle East, 49, 152–53
Miniter, Richard, 153
minority rights, 2
missile defense, 47
Mississippi, 56
Missouri, 20, 148
Mitchell, George, 178
Molinari, Susan, 158
Mondale, Walter, 21
Monroe, Marilyn, 170
Moore, Michael, 31
Moran, Mike, 64
Morris, Dick, 73, 108, 147; Hillary's
    ideology and, 110–13, 116; Hillary's
    private life and, 115; triangulation
    and, 173
Moscow, Russia, 118
Moseley Braun, Carol, 5
Motive, 123
Moynihan, Daniel Patrick, 20, 64, 65,
    136, 143; abortion and, 145; death
    of, 99–100; Hillary's health care
    plan and, 101–2; Hillary and,
    100–106; ideology of, 102–5; left
    and, 104–5; staff of, 25
Mr. Smith Goes to Washington, 56
Mugabe, Robert, 71
Myers, Lisa, 92

NAFTA. *See* North American Free Trade
    Agreement
NASA, 120
national security, 47
National Unitarian Convention, 119
NATO. *See* North Atlantic Treaty
    Organization
Neas, Ralph, 30
New Deal, 177
New Haven Legal Assistance
    Association, 128
New Jersey, 20, 31

New Mexico, 27, 148
New Orleans, La., 42
New Republic, 184
Newsmax, 154
Newsweek, 123
New York, 4, 5, 8
New Yorker, 37, 69, 155
New York Observer, 95–96
New York Post, 24, 47, 48, 49, 53
New York Stock Exchange, 61
New York Times, 11, 31, 68, 95, 171
New York Times Magazine, 109
New Zealand, 79
Nickles, Don, 41
Nixon, Richard M., 22, 46, 78, 82, 87,
    103, 104, 161–62, 176
Norquist, Grover, 197, 200
North American Free Trade Agreement
    (NAFTA), 173
North Atlantic Treaty Organization
    (NATO), 15, 177
North Carolina, 13, 36
North Dakota, 31
Novak, Robert, 44
NOW, 45
nuclear weapons, 49
Nunn, Sam, 194

O'Leary, Ann, 195
O'Reilly Factor, 32
Oglesby, Carl, 123
Olson, Barbara, 1–2, 90, 126, 130
Oneonta, N.Y., 40
Operation Iraqi Freedom, 48–50, 99,
    147
Orin, Deborah, 24, 49
Oslo Peace Accords, 152

Packwood, Robert, 176
Pakistan, 49
"The Paranoid Style in American
    Politics" (Hofstadter), 75
Pataki, George, 62, 64
Patriot Act, 199–200

peace, 2
Pelosi, Nancy, 24, 48
Penn, Mark, 81, 147
Pennsylvania, 148
penny-loafer conservatives, 6, 106–15
Pentagon, 15, 47
People for the American Way, 45
Percy, Walker, 115
perjury, 4
Phelan, James, 125
Pitney, John J., Jr., 138
Plunkitt, George Washington, 164
Podesta, John, 28–29
Podhoretz, Norman, 104
politics: of meaning, 107–9; of personal
    destruction, 5–6; rules of, 106–8
poverty, 101, 111
Powell, Colin, 49
The Prince (Machiavelli), 116
Progressive Policy Institute, 29

Quayle, Marilyn, 129
Quinn, Sally, 69
Quinnipiac University, 9

racism, 102
Rackley, Alex, 124
Ray, Robert, 74, 86, 88, 91–92
Reagan, Ronald, 19, 20, 89, 121, 147,
    165, 175, 177
Reeves, Thomas C., 169
Reich, Robert, 125
Reiner, Rob, 9, 31
Reines, Phillippe, 195
Reno, Janet, 30
Republican National Committee
    (RNC), 30
Republican Party: campaign finance
    and, 22–23; change in, 121; Clin-
    tons and, 162; conservatism and,
    29; Dean and, 137; Democratic
    Party vs., 180–85; health care and,
    13; Hillary and, 38–39, 44, 51–52;
    Hillary's criticism of, 13, 135–36;

Hillary's presidential ambitions
    and, 157–58; homeland security
    and, 13; Left-Behind America and,
    139, 140; Rockefeller wing of, 121;
    in Senate, 45; tax cuts and,
    133–36
Reveille for Radicals (Alinsky), 116
Rhodeen, Penn, 128–29
Rice, Condoleezza, 159
Rich, Denise, 95
Rich, Marc, 95
Richardson, Margaret Milner, 197
RNC. *See* Republican National
    Committee
Robespierre, 118
Rochester, N.Y., 116
Rockefeller, John D., 71, 121, 124
Rockefeller, John D., IV, 195
Rodham, Hugh, 67, 69, 95, 111, 122, 142
Roe v. Wade, 146
Romania, 146
Rometsch, Ellen, 169
Roosevelt, Eleanor, 70, 189, 191
Roosevelt, Franklin D., 21, 35, 48, 114,
    121, 166, 168, 169, 177, 189, 165
Roosevelt, Theodore, 21, 133, 165, 168
Rose Law Firm, 78, 111, 155
Rostenkowski, Dan, 179
Rostow, Eugene, 126
Rubin, Jerry, 125
Rubirosa, Profirio, 85
Rules for Radicals (Alinsky), 106, 107,
    112, 116
Russia. *See* Soviet Union
Rutherford, Skip, 14
Schlesinger, Arthur, Jr., 165
Schumer, Chuck: abortion and, 145;
    background of, 133; campaign
    finance and, 24; Hillary and, 60–62,
    155; Hillary on Steering Committee
    and, 45, 46; judicial nominations
    and, 58; Moynihan's death and, 100;
    tax cuts and, 133–34
Schwarzenegger, Arnold, 10, 144

Seale, Bobby, 125

Secret Service, 22, 38

Segal, Eli, 14

Senate: Armed Services Committee of, 15, 42–43, 46–50; co-sponsoring legislation in, 41; deaths in, 99–100; filibustering in, 55–59; Finance Committee of, 101; Hillary's 2006 reelection to, 13, 17, 62–65; Hillary in, 4, 5, 8, 35–65, 99–106; judicial nominations and, 55–59; Republican Conference Committee in, 45; Republican Party in, 45; rules of, 36–37, 42, 94–95; Steering and Coordination Committee of, 5, 25, 44–46; Whitewater and, 60

Senate Finance Committee, 101

Sentelle, David, 14

September 11, 10, 31, 37, 47–48, 50, 63; Bush and, 52, 53

Sharpton, Al, 5, 62–63, 147

Sheen, Martin, 9

Simon & Schuster, 67, 69

Sinclair, Upton, 116

Sklar, Richard, 14

Social Security, 135, 143

Solis Doyle, Patti, 195

Soros, George, 27, 28

Souljah, Sister, 146–47

Southampton, N.Y., 11

South Carolina, 56

Southeastern Legal Foundation, 88

Soviet Union, 49, 103

Spiegel, Der, 68

Spielberg, Steven, 9

Spitzer, Elliot, 62

Springsteen, Bruce, 63

Starr, Kenneth, 14, 73, 198; Clinton scandals and, 86–88; diabolizing of, 161, 168; McDougal's pardon and, 95; Whitewater and, 58

Starr Report, 87–88

Steering and Coordination Committee, Democratic, 5, 25, 44–46

Steinem, Gloria, 129

Stephanopoulos, George, 82

Stevenson, Adlai, 9, 19, 20

Stewart, Jimmy, 56

Stickin': The Case for Loyalty (Carville), 184

Stone, Roger, 62

Streisand, Barbra, 9

Studds, Gerry, 176

Sudan, 153–54, 206

Sweeney, John, 27

Symington, Stuart, 20

Syracuse Post-Standard, 40

Taft, Robert, 121

Taft, William Howard, 35

Taiwan, 49

tax cuts, 26, 133–36, 152

Teresa, Mother, 146

Terrell, Suzanne Haik, 41

Texas, 56

Texas, University of, 107, 108

Thatcher, Margaret, 205

Thomases, Susan, 8, 91, 155, 196

Thurmond, Strom, 44, 56, 71

Tikkun, 109

Tillich, Paul, 122

Time magazine, 101

Tinsley, Nikki, 52

Today Show, 52, 136

Torricelli, Robert, 20, 182

Travelgate, 74, 91–92, 96

Truman, Harry S., 21, 50, 121, 149, 153, 157, 177

Tyrrell, Patrick Daniel, 105

Tyson, Don, 90

Tyson Foods, 90

U.S. Supreme Court, 24, 146

United Mine Workers Union, 116

United Nations, 49, 102, 103

United States, 43, 102

United States Marine Corps, 3–4, 46–47

USA Today, 155

USS *Arizona*, 54

USS *Cole*, 153, 154

VandeHei, James, 28–29, 45
vast right-wing conspiracy, 32, 40, 75, 136, 193, 198
Vermont, 9
Vietnam, 119, 123, 167
Vilsack, Tom and Christie, 137, 148
Virginia, 47, 94
VTV, 31

Wall Street Journal, 74, 78, 199
Wallace, Henry, 50
Walters, Barbara, 39, 67, 75
Wartell, Sarah, 28
Washington Post, 28, 45, 81, 89, 95, 167, 194
Washington Research Project, 128
Washington Times, 31, 197, 199
Watergate, 87
Watkins, David, 91
Wattleton, Faye, 145
Wayne, John, 71
weapons of mass destruction, 49
Webster, Daniel, 100
Weekly Standard, 50
Wellesley, 6, 101, 113, 115, 123

Wellstone, Paul, 21
Wesley, John, 122
West Virginia, 56
Whitewater, 25, 58, 60, 74, 87–90, 95, 96
Wild Blue, The (Ambrose), 135
Willis, Bruce, 41
Wilson, Woodrow, 165, 166
Winston, Chriss, 32
Wisconsin, 59
Wolfson, Howard, 155, 195
women, 22
Woodward, Bob, 70
World Council of Churches, 121
Wright, Betsey, 83–84

Xerox, 138

Yale Law School, 6, 115, 118, 124, 127
Yale Review of Law and Social Action, 125
Yeltsin, Boris, 71

Zeifman, Jerome, 78–79
Zionism, 102